C-2113   CAREER EXAMINATION SERIES

*This is your
PASSBOOK for...*

Senior Building Inspector

*Test Preparation Study Guide
Questions & Answers*

COPYRIGHT NOTICE

This book is SOLELY intended for, is sold ONLY to, and its use is RESTRICTED to individual, bona fide applicants or candidates who qualify by virtue of having seriously filed applications for appropriate license, certificate, professional and/or promotional advancement, higher school matriculation, scholarship, or other legitimate requirements of education and/or governmental authorities.

This book is NOT intended for use, class instruction, tutoring, training, duplication, copying, reprinting, excerption, or adaptation, etc., by:

1) Other publishers
2) Proprietors and/or Instructors of "Coaching" and/or Preparatory Courses
3) Personnel and/or Training Divisions of commercial, industrial, and governmental organizations
4) Schools, colleges, or universities and/or their departments and staffs, including teachers and other personnel
5) Testing Agencies or Bureaus
6) Study groups which seek by the purchase of a single volume to copy and/or duplicate and/or adapt this material for use by the group as a whole without having purchased individual volumes for each of the members of the group
7) Et al.

Such persons would be in violation of appropriate Federal and State statutes.

PROVISION OF LICENSING AGREEMENTS – Recognized educational, commercial, industrial, and governmental institutions and organizations, and others legitimately engaged in educational pursuits, including training, testing, and measurement activities, may address request for a licensing agreement to the copyright owners, who will determine whether, and under what conditions, including fees and charges, the materials in this book may be used them. In other words, a licensing facility exists for the legitimate use of the material in this book on other than an individual basis. However, it is asseverated and affirmed here that the material in this book CANNOT be used without the receipt of the express permission of such a licensing agreement from the Publishers. Inquiries re licensing should be addressed to the company, attention rights and permissions department.

All rights reserved, including the right of reproduction in whole or in part, in any form or by any means, electronic or mechanical, including photocopying, recording, or by any information storage and retrieval system, without permission in writing from the Publisher.

Copyright © 2025 by
National Learning Corporation

212 Michael Drive, Syosset, NY 11791
(516) 921-8888 • www.passbooks.com
E-mail: info@passbooks.com

PASSBOOK® SERIES

THE *PASSBOOK® SERIES* has been created to prepare applicants and candidates for the ultimate academic battlefield – the examination room.

At some time in our lives, each and every one of us may be required to take an examination – for validation, matriculation, admission, qualification, registration, certification, or licensure.

Based on the assumption that every applicant or candidate has met the basic formal educational standards, has taken the required number of courses, and read the necessary texts, the *PASSBOOK® SERIES* furnishes the one special preparation which may assure passing with confidence, instead of failing with insecurity. Examination questions – together with answers – are furnished as the basic vehicle for study so that the mysteries of the examination and its compounding difficulties may be eliminated or diminished by a sure method.

This book is meant to help you pass your examination provided that you qualify and are serious in your objective.

The entire field is reviewed through the huge store of content information which is succinctly presented through a provocative and challenging approach – the question-and-answer method.

A climate of success is established by furnishing the correct answers at the end of each test.

You soon learn to recognize types of questions, forms of questions, and patterns of questioning. You may even begin to anticipate expected outcomes.

You perceive that many questions are repeated or adapted so that you can gain acute insights, which may enable you to score many sure points.

You learn how to confront new questions, or types of questions, and to attack them confidently and work out the correct answers.

You note objectives and emphases, and recognize pitfalls and dangers, so that you may make positive educational adjustments.

Moreover, you are kept fully informed in relation to new concepts, methods, practices, and directions in the field.

You discover that you are actually taking the examination all the time: you are preparing for the examination by "taking" an examination, not by reading extraneous and/or supererogatory textbooks.

In short, this PASSBOOK®, used directedly, should be an important factor in helping you to pass your test.

SENIOR BUILDING INSPECTOR

DUTIES
An employee in this class supervises the work of Building Inspectors by scheduling their daily activity and by reviewing the results of their work. In the absence of supervisory responsibilities, an employee in this class is responsible for the analysis and review, prior to the issuance of a building permit, of building plans and specifications for structural soundness and types of materials used. A significant part of the work is discussions held with contractors, builders and owners in regard to approval or disapproval of plans and the explanation of the building code in relationship to the plans submitted. Performs related work as required.

SCOPE OF THE EXAMINATION
The written test will be designed to test for knowledge, skills, and/or abilities in such areas as:
1. Inspection procedures and principles;
2. Methods and materials used in building construction and rehabilitation;
3. Understanding and interpreting building plans and requirements;
4. Building, housing and zoning laws and codes;
5. Preparing written material; and
6. Supervision.

HOW TO TAKE A TEST

I. YOU MUST PASS AN EXAMINATION

A. *WHAT EVERY CANDIDATE SHOULD KNOW*

Examination applicants often ask us for help in preparing for the written test. What can I study in advance? What kinds of questions will be asked? How will the test be given? How will the papers be graded?

As an applicant for a civil service examination, you may be wondering about some of these things. Our purpose here is to suggest effective methods of advance study and to describe civil service examinations.

Your chances for success on this examination can be increased if you know how to prepare. Those "pre-examination jitters" can be reduced if you know what to expect. You can even experience an adventure in good citizenship if you know why civil service exams are given.

B. *WHY ARE CIVIL SERVICE EXAMINATIONS GIVEN?*

Civil service examinations are important to you in two ways. As a citizen, you want public jobs filled by employees who know how to do their work. As a job seeker, you want a fair chance to compete for that job on an equal footing with other candidates. The best-known means of accomplishing this two-fold goal is the competitive examination.

Exams are widely publicized throughout the nation. They may be administered for jobs in federal, state, city, municipal, town or village governments or agencies.

Any citizen may apply, with some limitations, such as the age or residence of applicants. Your experience and education may be reviewed to see whether you meet the requirements for the particular examination. When these requirements exist, they are reasonable and applied consistently to all applicants. Thus, a competitive examination may cause you some uneasiness now, but it is your privilege and safeguard.

C. *HOW ARE CIVIL SERVICE EXAMS DEVELOPED?*

Examinations are carefully written by trained technicians who are specialists in the field known as "psychological measurement," in consultation with recognized authorities in the field of work that the test will cover. These experts recommend the subject matter areas or skills to be tested; only those knowledges or skills important to your success on the job are included. The most reliable books and source materials available are used as references. Together, the experts and technicians judge the difficulty level of the questions.

Test technicians know how to phrase questions so that the problem is clearly stated. Their ethics do not permit "trick" or "catch" questions. Questions may have been tried out on sample groups, or subjected to statistical analysis, to determine their usefulness.

Written tests are often used in combination with performance tests, ratings of training and experience, and oral interviews. All of these measures combine to form the best-known means of finding the right person for the right job.

II. HOW TO PASS THE WRITTEN TEST

A. NATURE OF THE EXAMINATION

To prepare intelligently for civil service examinations, you should know how they differ from school examinations you have taken. In school you were assigned certain definite pages to read or subjects to cover. The examination questions were quite detailed and usually emphasized memory. Civil service exams, on the other hand, try to discover your present ability to perform the duties of a position, plus your potentiality to learn these duties. In other words, a civil service exam attempts to predict how successful you will be. Questions cover such a broad area that they cannot be as minute and detailed as school exam questions.

In the public service similar kinds of work, or positions, are grouped together in one "class." This process is known as *position-classification*. All the positions in a class are paid according to the salary range for that class. One class title covers all of these positions, and they are all tested by the same examination.

B. FOUR BASIC STEPS

1) Study the announcement

How, then, can you know what subjects to study? Our best answer is: "Learn as much as possible about the class of positions for which you've applied." The exam will test the knowledge, skills and abilities needed to do the work.

Your most valuable source of information about the position you want is the official exam announcement. This announcement lists the training and experience qualifications. Check these standards and apply only if you come reasonably close to meeting them.

The brief description of the position in the examination announcement offers some clues to the subjects which will be tested. Think about the job itself. Review the duties in your mind. Can you perform them, or are there some in which you are rusty? Fill in the blank spots in your preparation.

Many jurisdictions preview the written test in the exam announcement by including a section called "Knowledge and Abilities Required," "Scope of the Examination," or some similar heading. Here you will find out specifically what fields will be tested.

2) Review your own background

Once you learn in general what the position is all about, and what you need to know to do the work, ask yourself which subjects you already know fairly well and which need improvement. You may wonder whether to concentrate on improving your strong areas or on building some background in your fields of weakness. When the announcement has specified "some knowledge" or "considerable knowledge," or has used adjectives like "beginning principles of…" or "advanced … methods," you can get a clue as to the number and difficulty of questions to be asked in any given field. More questions, and hence broader coverage, would be included for those subjects which are more important in the work. Now weigh your strengths and weaknesses against the job requirements and prepare accordingly.

3) Determine the level of the position

Another way to tell how intensively you should prepare is to understand the level of the job for which you are applying. Is it the entering level? In other words, is this the position in which beginners in a field of work are hired? Or is it an intermediate or advanced level? Sometimes this is indicated by such words as "Junior" or "Senior" in the class title. Other jurisdictions use Roman numerals to designate the level – Clerk I, Clerk II, for example. The word "Supervisor" sometimes appears in the title. If the level is not indicated by the title, check the description of duties. Will you be working under very close supervision, or will you have responsibility for independent decisions in this work?

4) Choose appropriate study materials

Now that you know the subjects to be examined and the relative amount of each subject to be covered, you can choose suitable study materials. For beginning level jobs, or even advanced ones, if you have a pronounced weakness in some aspect of your training, read a modern, standard textbook in that field. Be sure it is up to date and has general coverage. Such books are normally available at your library, and the librarian will be glad to help you locate one. For entry-level positions, questions of appropriate difficulty are chosen – neither highly advanced questions, nor those too simple. Such questions require careful thought but not advanced training.

If the position for which you are applying is technical or advanced, you will read more advanced, specialized material. If you are already familiar with the basic principles of your field, elementary textbooks would waste your time. Concentrate on advanced textbooks and technical periodicals. Think through the concepts and review difficult problems in your field.

These are all general sources. You can get more ideas on your own initiative, following these leads. For example, training manuals and publications of the government agency which employs workers in your field can be useful, particularly for technical and professional positions. A letter or visit to the government department involved may result in more specific study suggestions, and certainly will provide you with a more definite idea of the exact nature of the position you are seeking.

III. KINDS OF TESTS

Tests are used for purposes other than measuring knowledge and ability to perform specified duties. For some positions, it is equally important to test ability to make adjustments to new situations or to profit from training. In others, basic mental abilities not dependent on information are essential. Questions which test these things may not appear as pertinent to the duties of the position as those which test for knowledge and information. Yet they are often highly important parts of a fair examination. For very general questions, it is almost impossible to help you direct your study efforts. What we can do is to point out some of the more common of these general abilities needed in public service positions and describe some typical questions.

1) General information

Broad, general information has been found useful for predicting job success in some kinds of work. This is tested in a variety of ways, from vocabulary lists to questions about current events. Basic background in some field of work, such as sociology or economics, may be sampled in a group of questions. Often these are principles which have become familiar to most persons through exposure rather than through formal training. It is difficult to advise you how to study for these questions; being alert to the world around you is our best suggestion.

2) Verbal ability

An example of an ability needed in many positions is verbal or language ability. Verbal ability is, in brief, the ability to use and understand words. Vocabulary and grammar tests are typical measures of this ability. Reading comprehension or paragraph interpretation questions are common in many kinds of civil service tests. You are given a paragraph of written material and asked to find its central meaning.

3) Numerical ability

Number skills can be tested by the familiar arithmetic problem, by checking paired lists of numbers to see which are alike and which are different, or by interpreting charts and graphs. In the latter test, a graph may be printed in the test booklet which you are asked to use as the basis for answering questions.

4) Observation

A popular test for law-enforcement positions is the observation test. A picture is shown to you for several minutes, then taken away. Questions about the picture test your ability to observe both details and larger elements.

5) Following directions

In many positions in the public service, the employee must be able to carry out written instructions dependably and accurately. You may be given a chart with several columns, each column listing a variety of information. The questions require you to carry out directions involving the information given in the chart.

6) Skills and aptitudes

Performance tests effectively measure some manual skills and aptitudes. When the skill is one in which you are trained, such as typing or shorthand, you can practice. These tests are often very much like those given in business school or high school courses. For many of the other skills and aptitudes, however, no short-time preparation can be made. Skills and abilities natural to you or that you have developed throughout your lifetime are being tested.

Many of the general questions just described provide all the data needed to answer the questions and ask you to use your reasoning ability to find the answers. Your best preparation for these tests, as well as for tests of facts and ideas, is to be at your physical and mental best. You, no doubt, have your own methods of getting into an exam-taking mood and keeping "in shape." The next section lists some ideas on this subject.

IV. KINDS OF QUESTIONS

Only rarely is the "essay" question, which you answer in narrative form, used in civil service tests. Civil service tests are usually of the short-answer type. Full instructions for answering these questions will be given to you at the examination. But in case this is your first experience with short-answer questions and separate answer sheets, here is what you need to know:

1) Multiple-choice Questions

Most popular of the short-answer questions is the "multiple choice" or "best answer" question. It can be used, for example, to test for factual knowledge, ability to solve problems or judgment in meeting situations found at work.

A multiple-choice question is normally one of three types—
- It can begin with an incomplete statement followed by several possible endings. You are to find the one ending which *best* completes the statement, although some of the others may not be entirely wrong.
- It can also be a complete statement in the form of a question which is answered by choosing one of the statements listed.

- It can be in the form of a problem – again you select the best answer.

Here is an example of a multiple-choice question with a discussion which should give you some clues as to the method for choosing the right answer:

When an employee has a complaint about his assignment, the action which will *best* help him overcome his difficulty is to
- A. discuss his difficulty with his coworkers
- B. take the problem to the head of the organization
- C. take the problem to the person who gave him the assignment
- D. say nothing to anyone about his complaint

In answering this question, you should study each of the choices to find which is best. Consider choice "A" – Certainly an employee may discuss his complaint with fellow employees, but no change or improvement can result, and the complaint remains unresolved. Choice "B" is a poor choice since the head of the organization probably does not know what assignment you have been given, and taking your problem to him is known as "going over the head" of the supervisor. The supervisor, or person who made the assignment, is the person who can clarify it or correct any injustice. Choice "C" is, therefore, correct. To say nothing, as in choice "D," is unwise. Supervisors have and interest in knowing the problems employees are facing, and the employee is seeking a solution to his problem.

2) True/False Questions

The "true/false" or "right/wrong" form of question is sometimes used. Here a complete statement is given. Your job is to decide whether the statement is right or wrong.

SAMPLE: A roaming cell-phone call to a nearby city costs less than a non-roaming call to a distant city.

This statement is wrong, or false, since roaming calls are more expensive.

This is not a complete list of all possible question forms, although most of the others are variations of these common types. You will always get complete directions for answering questions. Be sure you understand *how* to mark your answers – ask questions until you do.

V. RECORDING YOUR ANSWERS

Computer terminals are used more and more today for many different kinds of exams.

For an examination with very few applicants, you may be told to record your answers in the test booklet itself. Separate answer sheets are much more common. If this separate answer sheet is to be scored by machine – and this is often the case – it is highly important that you mark your answers correctly in order to get credit.

An electronic scoring machine is often used in civil service offices because of the speed with which papers can be scored. Machine-scored answer sheets must be marked with a pencil, which will be given to you. This pencil has a high graphite content which responds to the electronic scoring machine. As a matter of fact, stray dots may register as answers, so do not let your pencil rest on the answer sheet while you are pondering the correct answer. Also, if your pencil lead breaks or is otherwise defective, ask for another.

Since the answer sheet will be dropped in a slot in the scoring machine, be careful not to bend the corners or get the paper crumpled.

The answer sheet normally has five vertical columns of numbers, with 30 numbers to a column. These numbers correspond to the question numbers in your test booklet. After each number, going across the page are four or five pairs of dotted lines. These short dotted lines have small letters or numbers above them. The first two pairs may also have a "T" or "F" above the letters. This indicates that the first two pairs only are to be used if the questions are of the true-false type. If the questions are multiple choice, disregard the "T" and "F" and pay attention only to the small letters or numbers.

Answer your questions in the manner of the sample that follows:

32. The largest city in the United States is
    A. Washington, D.C.
    B. New York City
    C. Chicago
    D. Detroit
    E. San Francisco

1) Choose the answer you think is best. (New York City is the largest, so "B" is correct.)
2) Find the row of dotted lines numbered the same as the question you are answering. (Find row number 32)
3) Find the pair of dotted lines corresponding to the answer. (Find the pair of lines under the mark "B.")
4) Make a solid black mark between the dotted lines.

VI. BEFORE THE TEST

Common sense will help you find procedures to follow to get ready for an examination. Too many of us, however, overlook these sensible measures. Indeed, nervousness and fatigue have been found to be the most serious reasons why applicants fail to do their best on civil service tests. Here is a list of reminders:

- Begin your preparation early – Don't wait until the last minute to go scurrying around for books and materials or to find out what the position is all about.
- Prepare continuously – An hour a night for a week is better than an all-night cram session. This has been definitely established. What is more, a night a week for a month will return better dividends than crowding your study into a shorter period of time.
- Locate the place of the exam – You have been sent a notice telling you when and where to report for the examination. If the location is in a different town or otherwise unfamiliar to you, it would be well to inquire the best route and learn something about the building.
- Relax the night before the test – Allow your mind to rest. Do not study at all that night. Plan some mild recreation or diversion; then go to bed early and get a good night's sleep.
- Get up early enough to make a leisurely trip to the place for the test – This way unforeseen events, traffic snarls, unfamiliar buildings, etc. will not upset you.
- Dress comfortably – A written test is not a fashion show. You will be known by number and not by name, so wear something comfortable.

- Leave excess paraphernalia at home – Shopping bags and odd bundles will get in your way. You need bring only the items mentioned in the official notice you received; usually everything you need is provided. Do not bring reference books to the exam. They will only confuse those last minutes and be taken away from you when in the test room.
- Arrive somewhat ahead of time – If because of transportation schedules you must get there very early, bring a newspaper or magazine to take your mind off yourself while waiting.
- Locate the examination room – When you have found the proper room, you will be directed to the seat or part of the room where you will sit. Sometimes you are given a sheet of instructions to read while you are waiting. Do not fill out any forms until you are told to do so; just read them and be prepared.
- Relax and prepare to listen to the instructions
- If you have any physical problem that may keep you from doing your best, be sure to tell the test administrator. If you are sick or in poor health, you really cannot do your best on the exam. You can come back and take the test some other time.

VII. AT THE TEST

The day of the test is here and you have the test booklet in your hand. The temptation to get going is very strong. Caution! There is more to success than knowing the right answers. You must know how to identify your papers and understand variations in the type of short-answer question used in this particular examination. Follow these suggestions for maximum results from your efforts:

1) Cooperate with the monitor

The test administrator has a duty to create a situation in which you can be as much at ease as possible. He will give instructions, tell you when to begin, check to see that you are marking your answer sheet correctly, and so on. He is not there to guard you, although he will see that your competitors do not take unfair advantage. He wants to help you do your best.

2) Listen to all instructions

Don't jump the gun! Wait until you understand all directions. In most civil service tests you get more time than you need to answer the questions. So don't be in a hurry. Read each word of instructions until you clearly understand the meaning. Study the examples, listen to all announcements and follow directions. Ask questions if you do not understand what to do.

3) Identify your papers

Civil service exams are usually identified by number only. You will be assigned a number; you must not put your name on your test papers. Be sure to copy your number correctly. Since more than one exam may be given, copy your exact examination title.

4) Plan your time

Unless you are told that a test is a "speed" or "rate of work" test, speed itself is usually not important. Time enough to answer all the questions will be provided, but this does not mean that you have all day. An overall time limit has been set. Divide the total time (in minutes) by the number of questions to determine the approximate time you have for each question.

5) Do not linger over difficult questions

If you come across a difficult question, mark it with a paper clip (useful to have along) and come back to it when you have been through the booklet. One caution if you do this – be sure to skip a number on your answer sheet as well. Check often to be sure that you have not lost your place and that you are marking in the row numbered the same as the question you are answering.

6) Read the questions

Be sure you know what the question asks! Many capable people are unsuccessful because they failed to *read* the questions correctly.

7) Answer all questions

Unless you have been instructed that a penalty will be deducted for incorrect answers, it is better to guess than to omit a question.

8) Speed tests

It is often better NOT to guess on speed tests. It has been found that on timed tests people are tempted to spend the last few seconds before time is called in marking answers at random – without even reading them – in the hope of picking up a few extra points. To discourage this practice, the instructions may warn you that your score will be "corrected" for guessing. That is, a penalty will be applied. The incorrect answers will be deducted from the correct ones, or some other penalty formula will be used.

9) Review your answers

If you finish before time is called, go back to the questions you guessed or omitted to give them further thought. Review other answers if you have time.

10) Return your test materials

If you are ready to leave before others have finished or time is called, take ALL your materials to the monitor and leave quietly. Never take any test material with you. The monitor can discover whose papers are not complete, and taking a test booklet may be grounds for disqualification.

VIII. EXAMINATION TECHNIQUES

1) Read the general instructions carefully. These are usually printed on the first page of the exam booklet. As a rule, these instructions refer to the timing of the examination; the fact that you should not start work until the signal and must stop work at a signal, etc. If there are any *special* instructions, such as a choice of questions to be answered, make sure that you note this instruction carefully.

2) When you are ready to start work on the examination, that is as soon as the signal has been given, read the instructions to each question booklet, underline any key words or phrases, such as *least, best, outline, describe* and the like. In this way you will tend to answer as requested rather than discover on reviewing your paper that you *listed without describing*, that you selected the *worst* choice rather than the *best* choice, etc.

3) If the examination is of the objective or multiple-choice type – that is, each question will also give a series of possible answers: A, B, C or D, and you are called upon to select the best answer and write the letter next to that answer on your answer paper – it is advisable to start answering each question in turn. There may be anywhere from 50 to 100 such questions in the three or four hours allotted and you can see how much time would be taken if you read through all the questions before beginning to answer any. Furthermore, if you come across a question or group of questions which you know would be difficult to answer, it would undoubtedly affect your handling of all the other questions.

4) If the examination is of the essay type and contains but a few questions, it is a moot point as to whether you should read all the questions before starting to answer any one. Of course, if you are given a choice – say five out of seven and the like – then it is essential to read all the questions so you can eliminate the two that are most difficult. If, however, you are asked to answer all the questions, there may be danger in trying to answer the easiest one first because you may find that you will spend too much time on it. The best technique is to answer the first question, then proceed to the second, etc.

5) Time your answers. Before the exam begins, write down the time it started, then add the time allowed for the examination and write down the time it must be completed, then divide the time available somewhat as follows:
    - If 3-1/2 hours are allowed, that would be 210 minutes. If you have 80 objective-type questions, that would be an average of 2-1/2 minutes per question. Allow yourself no more than 2 minutes per question, or a total of 160 minutes, which will permit about 50 minutes to review.
    - If for the time allotment of 210 minutes there are 7 essay questions to answer, that would average about 30 minutes a question. Give yourself only 25 minutes per question so that you have about 35 minutes to review.

6) The most important instruction is to *read each question* and make sure you know what is wanted. The second most important instruction is to *time yourself properly* so that you answer every question. The third most important instruction is to *answer every question*. Guess if you have to but include something for each question. Remember that you will receive no credit for a blank and will probably receive some credit if you write something in answer to an essay question. If you guess a letter – say "B" for a multiple-choice question – you may have guessed right. If you leave a blank as an answer to a multiple-choice question, the examiners may respect your feelings but it will not add a point to your score. Some exams may penalize you for wrong answers, so in such cases *only*, you may not want to guess unless you have some basis for your answer.

7) Suggestions
    a. Objective-type questions
        1. Examine the question booklet for proper sequence of pages and questions
        2. Read all instructions carefully
        3. Skip any question which seems too difficult; return to it after all other questions have been answered
        4. Apportion your time properly; do not spend too much time on any single question or group of questions

5. Note and underline key words – *all, most, fewest, least, best, worst, same, opposite,* etc.
6. Pay particular attention to negatives
7. Note unusual option, e.g., unduly long, short, complex, different or similar in content to the body of the question
8. Observe the use of "hedging" words – *probably, may, most likely,* etc.
9. Make sure that your answer is put next to the same number as the question
10. Do not second-guess unless you have good reason to believe the second answer is definitely more correct
11. Cross out original answer if you decide another answer is more accurate; do not erase until you are ready to hand your paper in
12. Answer all questions; guess unless instructed otherwise
13. Leave time for review

  b. Essay questions
    1. Read each question carefully
    2. Determine exactly what is wanted. Underline key words or phrases.
    3. Decide on outline or paragraph answer
    4. Include many different points and elements unless asked to develop any one or two points or elements
    5. Show impartiality by giving pros and cons unless directed to select one side only
    6. Make and write down any assumptions you find necessary to answer the questions
    7. Watch your English, grammar, punctuation and choice of words
    8. Time your answers; don't crowd material

8) Answering the essay question

Most essay questions can be answered by framing the specific response around several key words or ideas. Here are a few such key words or ideas:

M's: manpower, materials, methods, money, management
P's: purpose, program, policy, plan, procedure, practice, problems, pitfalls, personnel, public relations

  a. Six basic steps in handling problems:
    1. Preliminary plan and background development
    2. Collect information, data and facts
    3. Analyze and interpret information, data and facts
    4. Analyze and develop solutions as well as make recommendations
    5. Prepare report and sell recommendations
    6. Install recommendations and follow up effectiveness

  b. Pitfalls to avoid
    1. *Taking things for granted* – A statement of the situation does not necessarily imply that each of the elements is necessarily true; for example, a complaint may be invalid and biased so that all that can be taken for granted is that a complaint has been registered

2. *Considering only one side of a situation* – Wherever possible, indicate several alternatives and then point out the reasons you selected the best one
3. *Failing to indicate follow up* – Whenever your answer indicates action on your part, make certain that you will take proper follow-up action to see how successful your recommendations, procedures or actions turn out to be
4. *Taking too long in answering any single question* – Remember to time your answers properly

IX. AFTER THE TEST

Scoring procedures differ in detail among civil service jurisdictions although the general principles are the same. Whether the papers are hand-scored or graded by machine we have described, they are nearly always graded by number. That is, the person who marks the paper knows only the number – never the name – of the applicant. Not until all the papers have been graded will they be matched with names. If other tests, such as training and experience or oral interview ratings have been given, scores will be combined. Different parts of the examination usually have different weights. For example, the written test might count 60 percent of the final grade, and a rating of training and experience 40 percent. In many jurisdictions, veterans will have a certain number of points added to their grades.

After the final grade has been determined, the names are placed in grade order and an eligible list is established. There are various methods for resolving ties between those who get the same final grade – probably the most common is to place first the name of the person whose application was received first. Job offers are made from the eligible list in the order the names appear on it. You will be notified of your grade and your rank as soon as all these computations have been made. This will be done as rapidly as possible.

People who are found to meet the requirements in the announcement are called "eligibles." Their names are put on a list of eligible candidates. An eligible's chances of getting a job depend on how high he stands on this list and how fast agencies are filling jobs from the list.

When a job is to be filled from a list of eligibles, the agency asks for the names of people on the list of eligibles for that job. When the civil service commission receives this request, it sends to the agency the names of the three people highest on this list. Or, if the job to be filled has specialized requirements, the office sends the agency the names of the top three persons who meet these requirements from the general list.

The appointing officer makes a choice from among the three people whose names were sent to him. If the selected person accepts the appointment, the names of the others are put back on the list to be considered for future openings.

That is the rule in hiring from all kinds of eligible lists, whether they are for typist, carpenter, chemist, or something else. For every vacancy, the appointing officer has his choice of any one of the top three eligibles on the list. This explains why the person whose name is on top of the list sometimes does not get an appointment when some of the persons lower on the list do. If the appointing officer chooses the second or third eligible, the No. 1 eligible does not get a job at once, but stays on the list until he is appointed or the list is terminated.

X. HOW TO PASS THE INTERVIEW TEST

The examination for which you applied requires an oral interview test. You have already taken the written test and you are now being called for the interview test – the final part of the formal examination.

You may think that it is not possible to prepare for an interview test and that there are no procedures to follow during an interview. Our purpose is to point out some things you can do in advance that will help you and some good rules to follow and pitfalls to avoid while you are being interviewed.

What is an interview supposed to test?

The written examination is designed to test the technical knowledge and competence of the candidate; the oral is designed to evaluate intangible qualities, not readily measured otherwise, and to establish a list showing the relative fitness of each candidate – as measured against his competitors – for the position sought. Scoring is not on the basis of "right" and "wrong," but on a sliding scale of values ranging from "not passable" to "outstanding." As a matter of fact, it is possible to achieve a relatively low score without a single "incorrect" answer because of evident weakness in the qualities being measured.

Occasionally, an examination may consist entirely of an oral test – either an individual or a group oral. In such cases, information is sought concerning the technical knowledges and abilities of the candidate, since there has been no written examination for this purpose. More commonly, however, an oral test is used to supplement a written examination.

Who conducts interviews?

The composition of oral boards varies among different jurisdictions. In nearly all, a representative of the personnel department serves as chairman. One of the members of the board may be a representative of the department in which the candidate would work. In some cases, "outside experts" are used, and, frequently, a businessman or some other representative of the general public is asked to serve. Labor and management or other special groups may be represented. The aim is to secure the services of experts in the appropriate field.

However the board is composed, it is a good idea (and not at all improper or unethical) to ascertain in advance of the interview who the members are and what groups they represent. When you are introduced to them, you will have some idea of their backgrounds and interests, and at least you will not stutter and stammer over their names.

What should be done before the interview?

While knowledge about the board members is useful and takes some of the surprise element out of the interview, there is other preparation which is more substantive. It *is* possible to prepare for an oral interview – in several ways:

1) Keep a copy of your application and review it carefully before the interview

This may be the only document before the oral board, and the starting point of the interview. Know what education and experience you have listed there, and the sequence and dates of all of it. Sometimes the board will ask you to review the highlights of your experience for them; you should not have to hem and haw doing it.

2) Study the class specification and the examination announcement

Usually, the oral board has one or both of these to guide them. The qualities, characteristics or knowledges required by the position sought are stated in these documents. They offer valuable clues as to the nature of the oral interview. For example, if the job involves supervisory responsibilities, the announcement will usually indicate that knowledge of modern supervisory methods and the qualifications of the candidate as a supervisor will be tested. If so, you can expect such questions, frequently in the form of a hypothetical situation which you are expected to solve. NEVER go into an oral without knowledge of the duties and responsibilities of the job you seek.

3) Think through each qualification required

Try to visualize the kind of questions you would ask if you were a board member. How well could you answer them? Try especially to appraise your own knowledge and background in each area, *measured against the job sought*, and identify any areas in which you are weak. Be critical and realistic – do not flatter yourself.

4) Do some general reading in areas in which you feel you may be weak

For example, if the job involves supervision and your past experience has NOT, some general reading in supervisory methods and practices, particularly in the field of human relations, might be useful. Do NOT study agency procedures or detailed manuals. The oral board will be testing your understanding and capacity, not your memory.

5) Get a good night's sleep and watch your general health and mental attitude

You will want a clear head at the interview. Take care of a cold or any other minor ailment, and of course, no hangovers.

What should be done on the day of the interview?

Now comes the day of the interview itself. Give yourself plenty of time to get there. Plan to arrive somewhat ahead of the scheduled time, particularly if your appointment is in the fore part of the day. If a previous candidate fails to appear, the board might be ready for you a bit early. By early afternoon an oral board is almost invariably behind schedule if there are many candidates, and you may have to wait. Take along a book or magazine to read, or your application to review, but leave any extraneous material in the waiting room when you go in for your interview. In any event, relax and compose yourself.

The matter of dress is important. The board is forming impressions about you – from your experience, your manners, your attitude, and your appearance. Give your personal appearance careful attention. Dress your best, but not your flashiest. Choose conservative, appropriate clothing, and be sure it is immaculate. This is a business interview, and your appearance should indicate that you regard it as such. Besides, being well groomed and properly dressed will help boost your confidence.

Sooner or later, someone will call your name and escort you into the interview room. *This is it.* From here on you are on your own. It is too late for any more preparation. But remember, you asked for this opportunity to prove your fitness, and you are here because your request was granted.

What happens when you go in?

The usual sequence of events will be as follows: The clerk (who is often the board stenographer) will introduce you to the chairman of the oral board, who will introduce you to the other members of the board. Acknowledge the introductions before you sit down. Do not be surprised if you find a microphone facing you or a stenotypist sitting by. Oral interviews are usually recorded in the event of an appeal or other review.

Usually the chairman of the board will open the interview by reviewing the highlights of your education and work experience from your application – primarily for the benefit of the other members of the board, as well as to get the material into the record. Do not interrupt or comment unless there is an error or significant misinterpretation; if that is the case, do not hesitate. But do not quibble about insignificant matters. Also, he will usually ask you some question about your education, experience or your present job – partly to get you to start talking and to establish the interviewing "rapport." He may start the actual questioning, or turn it over to one of the other members. Frequently, each member undertakes the questioning on a particular area, one in which he is perhaps most competent, so you can expect each member to participate in the examination. Because time is limited, you may also expect some rather abrupt switches in the direction the questioning takes, so do not be upset by it. Normally, a board member will not pursue a single line of questioning unless he discovers a particular strength or weakness.

After each member has participated, the chairman will usually ask whether any member has any further questions, then will ask you if you have anything you wish to add. Unless you are expecting this question, it may floor you. Worse, it may start you off on an extended, extemporaneous speech. The board is not usually seeking more information. The question is principally to offer you a last opportunity to present further qualifications or to indicate that you have nothing to add. So, if you feel that a significant qualification or characteristic has been overlooked, it is proper to point it out in a sentence or so. Do not compliment the board on the thoroughness of their examination – they have been sketchy, and you know it. If you wish, merely say, "No thank you, I have nothing further to add." This is a point where you can "talk yourself out" of a good impression or fail to present an important bit of information. Remember, *you close the interview yourself*.

The chairman will then say, "That is all, Mr. _____, thank you." Do not be startled; the interview is over, and quicker than you think. Thank him, gather your belongings and take your leave. Save your sigh of relief for the other side of the door.

How to put your best foot forward

Throughout this entire process, you may feel that the board individually and collectively is trying to pierce your defenses, seek out your hidden weaknesses and embarrass and confuse you. Actually, this is not true. They are obliged to make an appraisal of your qualifications for the job you are seeking, and they want to see you in your best light. Remember, they must interview all candidates and a non-cooperative candidate may become a failure in spite of their best efforts to bring out his qualifications. Here are 15 suggestions that will help you:

1) **Be natural – Keep your attitude confident, not cocky**

    If you are not confident that you can do the job, do not expect the board to be. Do not apologize for your weaknesses, try to bring out your strong points. The board is interested in a positive, not negative, presentation. Cockiness will antagonize any board member and make him wonder if you are covering up a weakness by a false show of strength.

2) **Get comfortable, but don't lounge or sprawl**

    Sit erectly but not stiffly. A careless posture may lead the board to conclude that you are careless in other things, or at least that you are not impressed by the importance of the occasion. Either conclusion is natural, even if incorrect. Do not fuss with your clothing, a pencil or an ashtray. Your hands may occasionally be useful to emphasize a point; do not let them become a point of distraction.

3) **Do not wisecrack or make small talk**

    This is a serious situation, and your attitude should show that you consider it as such. Further, the time of the board is limited – they do not want to waste it, and neither should you.

4) Do not exaggerate your experience or abilities

In the first place, from information in the application or other interviews and sources, the board may know more about you than you think. Secondly, you probably will not get away with it. An experienced board is rather adept at spotting such a situation, so do not take the chance.

5) If you know a board member, do not make a point of it, yet do not hide it

Certainly you are not fooling him, and probably not the other members of the board. Do not try to take advantage of your acquaintanceship – it will probably do you little good.

6) Do not dominate the interview

Let the board do that. They will give you the clues – do not assume that you have to do all the talking. Realize that the board has a number of questions to ask you, and do not try to take up all the interview time by showing off your extensive knowledge of the answer to the first one.

7) Be attentive

You only have 20 minutes or so, and you should keep your attention at its sharpest throughout. When a member is addressing a problem or question to you, give him your undivided attention. Address your reply principally to him, but do not exclude the other board members.

8) Do not interrupt

A board member may be stating a problem for you to analyze. He will ask you a question when the time comes. Let him state the problem, and wait for the question.

9) Make sure you understand the question

Do not try to answer until you are sure what the question is. If it is not clear, restate it in your own words or ask the board member to clarify it for you. However, do not haggle about minor elements.

10) Reply promptly but not hastily

A common entry on oral board rating sheets is "candidate responded readily," or "candidate hesitated in replies." Respond as promptly and quickly as you can, but do not jump to a hasty, ill-considered answer.

11) Do not be peremptory in your answers

A brief answer is proper – but do not fire your answer back. That is a losing game from your point of view. The board member can probably ask questions much faster than you can answer them.

12) Do not try to create the answer you think the board member wants

He is interested in what kind of mind you have and how it works – not in playing games. Furthermore, he can usually spot this practice and will actually grade you down on it.

13) Do not switch sides in your reply merely to agree with a board member

Frequently, a member will take a contrary position merely to draw you out and to see if you are willing and able to defend your point of view. Do not start a debate, yet do not surrender a good position. If a position is worth taking, it is worth defending.

14) Do not be afraid to admit an error in judgment if you are shown to be wrong

The board knows that you are forced to reply without any opportunity for careful consideration. Your answer may be demonstrably wrong. If so, admit it and get on with the interview.

15) Do not dwell at length on your present job

The opening question may relate to your present assignment. Answer the question but do not go into an extended discussion. You are being examined for a *new* job, not your present one. As a matter of fact, try to phrase ALL your answers in terms of the job for which you are being examined.

Basis of Rating

Probably you will forget most of these "do's" and "don'ts" when you walk into the oral interview room. Even remembering them all will not ensure you a passing grade. Perhaps you did not have the qualifications in the first place. But remembering them will help you to put your best foot forward, without treading on the toes of the board members.

Rumor and popular opinion to the contrary notwithstanding, an oral board wants you to make the best appearance possible. They know you are under pressure – but they also want to see how you respond to it as a guide to what your reaction would be under the pressures of the job you seek. They will be influenced by the degree of poise you display, the personal traits you show and the manner in which you respond.

ABOUT THIS BOOK

This book contains tests divided into Examination Sections. Go through each test, answering every question in the margin. We have also attached a sample answer sheet at the back of the book that can be removed and used. At the end of each test look at the answer key and check your answers. On the ones you got wrong, look at the right answer choice and learn. Do not fill in the answers first. Do not memorize the questions and answers, but understand the answer and principles involved. On your test, the questions will likely be different from the samples. Questions are changed and new ones added. If you understand these past questions you should have success with any changes that arise. Tests may consist of several types of questions. We have additional books on each subject should more study be advisable or necessary for you. Finally, the more you study, the better prepared you will be. This book is intended to be the last thing you study before you walk into the examination room. Prior study of relevant texts is also recommended. NLC publishes some of these in our Fundamental Series. Knowledge and good sense are important factors in passing your exam. Good luck also helps. So now study this Passbook, absorb the material contained within and take that knowledge into the examination. Then do your best to pass that exam.

EXAMINATION SECTION

EXAMINATION SECTION
TEST 1

DIRECTIONS: Each question or incomplete statement is followed by several suggested answers or completions. Select the one that BEST answers the question or completes the statement. *PRINT THE LETTER OF THE CORRECT ANSWER IN THE SPACE AT THE RIGHT.*

1. Of the following reasons for inspection of construction, the one that applies MOST to inspectors in the department is to

   A. coordinate work of the different crafts
   B. avoid extra construction costs
   C. insure adherence to standards of materials and craftsmanship
   D. speed completion of the work

   1.____

2. Of the following statements, the one that is CORRECT is that it is

   A. not important for an inspector to maintain good, personal relations with contractors because contractors might attempt to take advantage of the inspector
   B. important for an inspector to maintain good personal relations with contractors because it will then be easier to obtain cooperation from them
   C. not important for an inspector to maintain good personal relations with contractors because contractors must comply with the Code in any case
   D. important for an inspector to maintain good personal relations with contractors because the inspector can then eliminate much of the required inspections

   2.____

3. Contractors will many times insist on discussing problems only with the senior construction inspector rather than the district inspector.
   This practice is

   A. *good,* because the contractor will get the correct answer immediately
   B. *poor,* because it tends to undermine the responsibility of the district inspector
   C. *good,* because this gives the senior construction inspector an opportunity to train the men under him
   D. *poor,* because the senior construction inspector cannot be familiar with all the conditions in his area.

   3.____

4. It has been said that the perfect job has never been built. Where litigation with respect to a job arises, the BEST indications that the inspector has made proper inspections are the

   A. statements made by the builder
   B. inspector's district assignments
   C. number of violations filed in a district
   D. inspector's written reports

   4.____

5. Defective material should be removed from the job site immediately.
   The MAIN reason for this is to

   A. prevent accidents due to poor *housekeeping*
   B. prevent *accidental* use of the defective material in the construction

   5.____

1

C. protect the department from any claim against the department
D. insure that the builder does not make the same mistake again

6. A senior inspector should always explain to newly appointed inspectors the importance of the work to be done by them. The MAIN reason for this is that

   A. the inspectors know what has to be done
   B. if this is not done, inspectors will skip unimportant inspections
   C. an inspector who understands the value of proper inspections will most likely do a better job
   D. inspectors will then not have an excuse for making improper inspections

7. Assume that you find that the inspections and reports made by a newly appointed inspector are consistently below a reasonable standard.
You should FIRST

   A. ask that the inspector be reassigned to a task he can perform properly
   B. request that the inspector be brought up on charges
   C. prepare a formal memorandum stating the facts so that your superiors will be aware of the situation
   D. try to determine and correct the cause for the sub-standard performance

8. In introducing new policies to inspectors under them, senior inspectors should

   A. describe the new policy in detail to each man individually so that the senior is sure the man knows it
   B. describe the new policy to the men and explain the necessity of the new policy
   C. tell the men your honest opinion of the policy, but also tell them it is the department's orders and must be followed
   D. give the men the new policy in writing so that there can be no excuse that they misunderstood you

9. Cooperation from inspectors working under you can BEST be secured by

   A. siding with the inspectors whenever they have a complaint
   B. being a stern disciplinarian and not letting the inspectors get away with anything
   C. emphasizing to the inspectors that if they want anything done for them, they must come to you
   D. being willing to listen to the inspectors, and helping them where possible

10. It is considered good practice for a supervisor to encourage his subordinates to discuss and participate in the solution of problems.
The MAIN reason for this is that

    A. the subordinate generally knows more about the individual problem than the supervisor
    B. then two people can share the responsibility instead of only one
    C. this will Increase the job satisfaction of the men and improve morale
    D. it will reduce the work load of the supervisor so that he can spend more time on more important matters

11. Of the following, the one MOST important quality required of a good supervisor is 11.____

    A. ambition B. leadership C. friendliness D. popularity

12. When an inspector submits a poorly written report, the senior inspector should 12.____

    A. discuss the report with the inspector as soon as possible after it has been submitted
    B. call a meeting of all inspectors to explain how reports should be written
    C. wait a few days to see if other reports turned in by the inspector are written the same way
    D. rewrite the report properly himself

13. A senior inspector who is very lenient with his men will find A senior inspector who is very lenient with his men will find that 13.____

    A. the men will cooperate more readily with him
    B. there will be a higher quality of performance from the men
    C. the men will have less respect for the senior inspector
    D. the men will get along better among themselves

14. It is often said that a supervisor can delegate authority, but never responsibility. This means MOST NEARLY that 14.____

    A. a supervisor must do his own work if he expects it to be done properly
    B. a supervisor can assign some one else to do his work, but in the last analysis, the supervisor himself must take the blame for any actions followed
    C. authority and responsibility are two separate things that cannot be borne by the same person
    D. it is better for a supervisor never to delegate his authority

15. Of the following, the MOST important characteristic of a good senior inspector is 15.____

    A. the ability to make friends with the men under him
    B. fairness in dealing with the men under him
    C. willingness to be on the men's side in their complaints against the Department
    D. willingness to overlook mistakes made by the men under him

16. The BEST relationship between the senior inspector and his inspectors exist when 16.____

    A. they stick together against adverse criticism made by the department heads
    B. the senior inspector respects the inspectors' rights
    C. the senior inspector will *cover* for the inspectors' faults
    D. the senior inspector avoids enforcing the rules he knows the men do not like

17. With regard to public relations, the MOST important item should be emphasized in an employee training program is that 17.____

    A. each inspector is a public relations agent
    B. an inspector should give the public all the information it asks for
    C. it is better to make mistakes and give erroneous information then to tell the public that you do not know the correct answer to their problem
    D. public relations is so specialized a field that only persons specially trained in it should consider it

18. Senior inspectors should regularly visit the districts covered by the inspectors under them in order to

    A. make sure their inspectors know that they are being watched
    B. give people an opportunity to speak directly to the *person in charge*
    C. observe the work of their inspectors to see that they meet proper standards
    D. get the public acquainted with them

19. The one of the following statements that is CORRECT is:

    A. When a stupid question is asked of you by the public, it should be disregarded.
    B. If you insist on formality between you and the public, the public will not be able to ask stupid questions that cannot be answered.
    C. The public should be treated courteously, regardless of how stupid their questions may be.
    D. You should explain to the public how stupid their questions are.

20. Assume that during field inspections, senior inspectors are constantly being asked questions about their job.
    In this respect, the inspector should remember that

    A. entering into conversation with people not connected with the job will leave the impression that city employees do little work
    B. efficiency can best be demonstrated by appearing to be too busy to answer questions
    C. supervisors should take every opportunity to tell the public how busy they really are
    D. the attitudes of the public are often formed by their personal contact's with city employees

21. The condition MOST likely to improve the morale of the inspectional force is

    A. liberal time allowances
    B. recognition of each individual's own efforts by the department
    C. overlooking of minor infractions of rules
    D. allowing the men to do the job in whatever manner they feel proper

22. As a senior inspector, you find that, in error you have reprimanded one of your inspectors.
    You should

    A. ignore the error, but be more careful in the future
    B. make up for it in the future by ignoring his next mistake
    C. find something else wrong
    D. apologize to the man for your mistake

23. As a senior inspector, assume that you have to settle a complaint made by a property owner against one of your inspectors. The PROPER thing to do would be to

    A. back up your inspector, telling the owner he is wrong
    B. tell the owner you will protect him against unjustified violations
    C. listen to both inspector and owner to get at the truth
    D. tell the owner you will check into the matter at your earliest convenience

24. Assume a suggestion is made by one of your inspectors for improving inspectional procedures.
    Of the following, the BEST course to follow is to

    A. tell the inspector that the present method used has always been followed and is therefore the best way
    B. check the inspector's suggestion, and if it is good pass it on to the chief inspector
    C. have the man write a report to the superintendent with regard to the suggestion
    D. hold a meeting with the other inspectors to see whether they like the suggestion

25. With respect to anonymous complaints, it is

    A. *good practice* to investigate them since they may be valid
    B. *poor practice* to investigate them since anyone who is not honest enough to sign his name is probably just a trouble maker
    C. *good practice* to investigate them to keep your inspectors *on their toes*
    D. *poor practice* to investigate them since this gives your inspectors the feeling they are being spied upon

26. Members of the public frequently ask about departmental procedures.
    Of the following, it is BEST to

    A. advise the public to put the question in writing so that he can get a proper formal reply
    B. refuse to answer, because this is a confidential matter
    C. explain the procedure as briefly as possible
    D. attempt to avoid the issue by discussing other matters

27. In making an inspection on an alteration job, you should

    A. avoid conversation with the foreman on the job
    B. try to get the foreman to talk as much as possible so that he will tell you all the things that are wrong with the job
    C. give the appearance of listening to the foreman but actually ignoring most of what he says
    D. listen to what the foreman has to say, but discourage undue conversation

28. Of the following, the one that would LEAST likely occur as a result of planning of your work is

    A. anticipation of problems before they occur
    B. necessity of frequently putting in overtime to solve problems
    C. better job coordination
    D. ability to meet deadlines for reports

29. In evaluating the quality of an inspector, a senior inspector should be LEAST interested in

    A. whether the man is adaptable to different situations
    B. the man's dependability
    C. how the man gets along with his co-workers and the public
    D. the number of reports the man turns in

30. In instituting disciplinary action against an inspector, the senior inspector should avoid 30._____
    A. taking extenuating circumstances into account
    B. explaining the serious consequences of the infraction
    C. being firm and positive
    D. delay once a decision is reached

KEY (CORRECT ANSWERS)

1.	C	16.	B
2.	B	17.	A
3.	B	18.	C
4.	D	19.	C
5.	B	20.	D
6.	C	21.	B
7.	D	22.	D
8.	B	23.	C
9.	D	24.	B
10.	C	25.	A
11.	B	26.	C
12.	A	27.	D
13.	C	28.	B
14.	B	29.	D
15.	B	30.	D

EXAMINATION SECTION
TEST 1

DIRECTIONS: Each question or incomplete statement is followed by several suggested answers or completions. Select the one that BEST answers the questions or completes the statement. *PRINT THE LETTER OF THE CORRECT ANSWER IN THE SPACE AT THE RIGHT.*

1. Of the following, the FIRST operation in the demolition of a 4-story building adjacent to the property line is the

    A. erection of railings around the stairwells
    B. shoring of adjoining buildings
    C. erection of a sidewalk shed
    D. removal of windows

    1.____

2. Projected sash is defined as a(n)

    A. double hung window
    B. window that opens inward or outward
    C. architectural projection from a building exterior
    D. storm window

    2.____

3. Specifications for a reinforced concrete structure call for a roof fill to be placed on the concrete roof slab. Of the following, the PURPOSE of the fill is to

    A. reduce sound transmission
    B. facilitate drainage
    C. provide a smooth base for insulation
    D. protect the concrete slab

    3.____

4. The Building Department requires a location survey by a licensed surveyor

    A. *only* if it is suspected that the building is not in the proper place and may impinge on adjacent property
    B. *only* of the completed foundation
    C. *only* of the completed superstructure
    D. *after* the foundation is completed and a second survey after the building is completed

    4.____

5. After excavating by a contractor for a footing, the sub-grade soil appears to be below the quality shown on the borings.
   Of the following types of footings, the one that would be LEAST affected by this condition is a

    A. spread footing   B. combined footing
    C. footing on piles   D. footing and pier

    5.____

6. Of the following, the information of GREATEST significance to be recorded for each pile during pile driving is the

    A. steam pressure and the temperature
    B. condition of the ground at the pile location

    6.____

C. number of hammer blows at the last inch
D. total number of hammer blows

7. One method of dewatering an excavation for a foundation is by the use of

   A. inverted siphons
   B. well points
   C. line holes
   D. suction heads

8. An excavation for a concrete footing to support a structural steel column was dug 4" too deep.
   Of the following, the BEST construction practice would be to

   A. backfill the 4" with stone
   B. backfill the 4" with sand
   C. lower the entire footing 4"
   D. make the footing 4" thicker

9. Spudding, in a pile driving operation, is used PRIMARILY to

   A. remove a broken pile
   B. pass an obstruction
   C. compact the soil in the area
   D. splice piles

10. Where walers and form ties are used in wood formwork for tall vertical concrete walls, the walers are

    A. more closely spaced at the top of the wall than at the bottom
    B. evenly spaced at the top to the bottom of the wall
    C. more closely spaced at the bottom of the wall than at the top
    D. more closely spaced at the middle of the wall than at either the top or the bottom

11. A non-bearing wall unit between columns enclosing a structure is known as a _____ wall.

    A. panel
    B. curtain
    C. apron
    D. spandrel

12. In a multi-story building, standpipes are installed FIRST by the plumber for

    A. water supply
    B. sanitary facilities
    C. fire protection
    D. steam supply

13. It is necessary to burn reinforcing steel while they are in the wood forms in order to change their lengths.
    The STANDARD safety precaution to observe during this process is to

    A. fireproof the wood forms
    B. use a low heat flame
    C. have a man stand by with a fire extinguisher
    D. soak a 20-foot radius around the area with water

14. Specifications for a building require that the first floor beams must be in place before backfilling against the foundation walls.
    Of the following, the BEST reason for this requirement is that

    A. the utilities up to the first floor level should be in place before backfilling
    B. without the first floor beams in place, the wall may become overstressed
    C. it facilitates the inspection of the first floor construction
    D. it facilitates the inspection of the backfilling operation

15. The utility line that USUALLY enters the building at the *lowest* elevation is the

    A. electric cable
    B. gas lines
    C. water lines
    D. plumbing drain

16. Specifications for a building require that machine excavation for foundation footings be within a foot of final subgrade and the remaining excavation be done by hand. Of the following, the BEST reasons for this requirement is to

    A. prevent cave-ins around the excavation
    B. save the amount of fill needed
    C. prevent disturbing the surrounding excavation
    D. prevent excavation below the subgrade

17. Of the following outside lines entering a building, the one for which grades must be MOST carefully controlled is the

    A. sewer line
    B. water line
    C. gas line
    D. electric cable

18. On a plan, the grades for a building are as follows:
    Datum ± 0 (Elev. 24.08')
    First floor El + 1' - 0" (Elev. 25.08').
    The elevation of a ledge 6'3" below the finished first floor level with respect to datum is

    A. El. - 6.25
    B. El. - 5.25
    C. El. + 18.83
    D. El. + 17.83

19. Specifications for a building call for *defective material to be removed from the job site immediately.* The MAIN reason for this is to

    A. prevent accidents
    B. prevent accidental use of the defective material in the construction
    C. insure that the contractor does not make the same mistake again
    D. minimize claims against the department

20. *Drywall* is installed by

    A. carpenters
    B. lathers
    C. plasterers
    D. masons

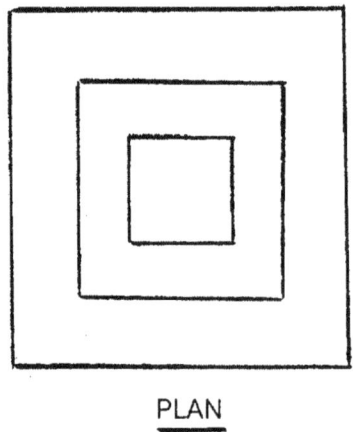

PLAN

21. The Plan of a footing and concrete column is shown above. An elevation of the footing would be shown as: 21.____

A. 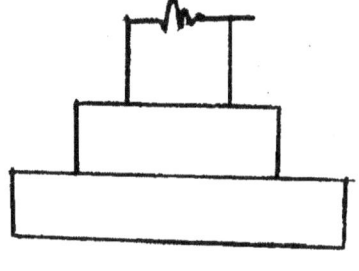   B.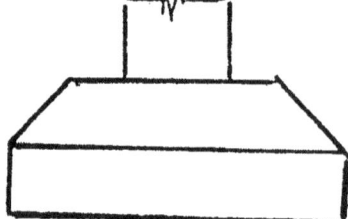

C. 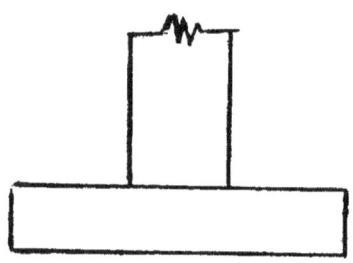   D.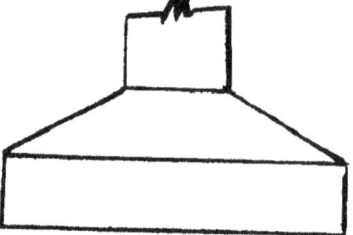

22. Of the following, the BEST sequence to follow in pouring the interior footing, concrete column and basement floor as shown below is pour the footing, 22.____

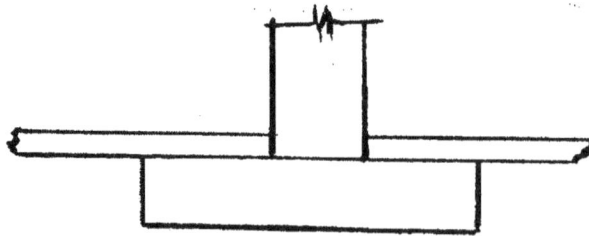

A. and floor in one pour. Pour the column
B. and column in one pour. Pour the floor
C. pour the floor above the footing, pour the column above the floor
D. box out for the floor, pour the column. Pour the floor

23. The PURPOSE of curing concrete is so that the   23.____

    A. forms for the concrete can be stripped quickly
    B. water content will not evaporate too quickly
    C. concrete will harden faster
    D. reinforcing rods will not rust

24. Air-entraining cement may be required so that the resulting concrete will resist   24.____

    A. freezing and thawing   B. hot weather
    C. dampness   D. heavy loads

25. Concrete test cylinders are required to   25.____

    A. provide an indication of the strength of the concrete poured in a specific location
    B. provide a basis of payment
    C. check on the inspector
    D. check the source of material

26. Concrete test cylinders are stored and cured on the job   26.____

    A. so that the contractor can then control the curing
    B. so that the inspector can then control the curing
    C. because the laboratory has no facilities for curing concrete cylinders
    D. because conditions of curing on the job are the same as at the location poured

27. The *water-cement ratio* refers to the quantity of water in a concrete mix as   27.____

    A. cubic feet of water per cubic foot of cement
    B. gallons of water per pound of cement
    C. gallons of water per sack of cement
    D. bags of cement per gallon of water

28. *Slump* of concrete refers to the   28.____

    A. shrinkage of concrete while setting
    B. drop in height relative to a standard testing cone
    C. amount of water introduced into the concrete
    D. cracking or crazing of the surface of concrete

29. Concrete mixes made with lightweight aggregate USUALLY require the addition of an air-   29.____
    entraining agent in order to

    A. increase the strength of the concrete
    B. reduce the weight of the concrete
    C. obtain the necessary plasticity without added water
    D. save aggregate material

30. Concrete in some instances requires integral waterproofing.   30.____
    This can BEST be achieved by

    A. addition of more cement in the mix
    B. longer vibration
    C. addition of a waterproofing agent to the mix
    D. longer curing period

31. In placing concrete where the vertical drop is greater than 5 feet, the use of an elephant trunk is necessary.
The BEST reason for using an elephant trunk is to

    A. prevent segregation of the aggregate
    B. prevent waste of material
    C. safeguard health and property
    D. save time and labor

32. According to the Building Code, the maximum size of coarse aggregate for reinforced concrete shall be one-fifth of the narrowest dimension between forms or three-quarters of the clear spacing between reinforcing bars. Of the following, the MAXIMUM sized aggregate permitted for a 12" wall with #6 bars spaced at 3" center to center is

    A. 1 3/4"   B. 1 1/2"   C. 1 1/4"   D. 1"

33. Of the following, the one that is NOT a name for a lightweight aggregate is

    A. Solite   B. Vitralite
    C. Lelite   D. Nitralite

34. High early strength cement is designated as

    A. Type I   B. Type II   C. Type III   D. Type IV

35. The average weight of stone concrete is, MOST NEARLY, _____ lb./cu. ft.

    A. 125   B. 150
    C. 175   D. 200

KEY (CORRECT ANSWERS)

1. C
2. B
3. B
4. D
5. C

6. C
7. B
8. D
9. B
10. C

11. B
12. C
13. C
14. B
15. D

16. D
17. A
18. B
19. B
20. A

21. A
22. D
23. B
24. A
25. A

26. D
27. C
28. B
29. C
30. C

31. A
32. B
33. B
34. C
35. B

TEST 2

DIRECTIONS: Each question or incomplete statement is followed by several suggested answers or completions. Select the one that BEST answers the question or completes the statement. *PRINT THE LETTER OF THE CORRECT ANSWER IN THE SPACE AT THE RIGHT.*

1. The Building Code requires that concrete shall be kept in a moist condition, after placing, for at least the FIRST _____ days.   1._____

    A. 3   B. 7   C. 14   D. 28

2. In concrete work, a dummy joint is SIMILAR in purpose to a(n) _____ joint.   2._____

    A. expansion
    B. construction
    C. contraction
    D. shear

3. Specifications for concrete usually contain a statement disallowing the *retampering* of concrete. *Retampering* means   3._____

    A. adding more water to the drum after ingredients are mixed
    B. vibrating of concrete in the forms
    C. mixing of the remaining concrete after some concrete is taken from the truck
    D. mixing of concrete in the truck after it has partially set and adding water

4. Chamfers are placed on a concrete beam PRIMARILY to   4._____

    A. save weight
    B. eliminate honeycomb
    C. eliminate sharp corners
    D. save construction costs

5. Of the following, the BEST reason for using vibrators in concrete construction is to   5._____

    A. increase the workability of the concrete
    B. consolidate the concrete
    C. slow up the setting
    D. speed up the setting

6. The concrete test that will BEST determine the consistency of a concrete mix is the   6._____

    A. sieve analysis
    B. water-cement ratio test
    C. calorimetric test
    D. slump test

7. Specifications for the concrete floor treatment of a building require *dustproofing*. This process consists of   7._____

    A. scraping the floor surface to remove loose concrete material that will dust
    B. mopping the floor with a chemical solution that will harden the concrete surface
    C. adding a chemical compound to the concrete mix that will harden the surface of the concrete
    D. grinding the concrete floor with a terrazzo machine that will case harden the surface of the concrete

8. In checking the placement of reinforcing steel, it is discovered that reinforcing steel called for on the design drawings is not shown on the reinforcing steel shop drawings. Of the following, the BEST procedure to follow is to   8._____

A. check the design drawings for the errors
B. check the shop drawings for the errors
C. subtract the missing steel in the field
D. stop all work

9. While a large spread footing of about 50 cubic yards Is being poured, the supply plant breaks down. Concrete is available from another supplier.
The use of the other supplier should

   A. not be approved because the supplier may not be approved
   B. be approved since additional test cylinders can be taken
   C. not be approved since construction joints can be installed where the pour has ended
   D. be approved as the concrete in footings is relatively unimportant

10. Of the following species of lumber, the one MOST likely to be used for concrete formwork is

    A. oak   B. pine   C. maple   D. birch

11. A contractor proposes to install the roofing two days after the concrete roof slab is poured.
This proposal should

    A. *be recommended* as it will speed the construction
    B. *be recommended* as it will cure the concrete better
    C. *not be recommended* as excess water may bulge the roofing
    D. *not be recommended* in cold weather but would be recommended in warm weather

12. For the construction of concrete floors resting on earth, the item that should be MOST carefully checked is that

    A. the earth is dry before pouring
    B. the earth is wet before pouring
    C. all backfill is properly compacted
    D. all backfill is porous soil

13. Cracks in concrete are not necessarily caused by settlement of a structure. Sometimes they are caused by

    A. shrinkage   B. plastic flow
    C. hydration   D. curing

14. Specifications for a building state that reinforcing bars must lap 40 diameters in the concrete.
The length of lap for a number 6 bar should be, MOST NEARLY, _____ inches.

    A. 12   B. 20   C. 30   D. 40

15. Cement stored on the job site that has become caked and lumpy may

    A. be used only for foundations
    B. be used only for slabs on ground
    C. be used anywhere if the lumps are broken up
    D. not be used

16. Of the following statements relating to the plies in plywood, the one that is CORRECT is: 16.____
    A. The primary difference between exterior and interior plywood is the quality of the exterior plies.
    B. Exterior plywood has more plies than interior plywood.
    C. Exterior plywood has no surface defects on the outer plies while interior plywood permits surface defects on the outer plies.
    D. Plywood has an odd number of plies.

17. Of the following, the one that is NOT a principal classification of lumber according to the American Lumber Standards is 17.____
    A. building   B. structural
    C. yard   D. shop

18. Of the following types of lumber, the one that is classified as a hardwood is 18.____
    A. cedar   B. fir   C. pine   D. maple

19. When building the formwork for a 12" doubly reinforced concrete wall, the USUAL order of conctruction is to place the 19.____
    A. formwork for both faces of the wall; then place the steel
    B. formwork for one face of the wall, place all reinforcing steel, then place the form-work for the other face of the wall
    C. reinforcing steel, then place the formwork for both faces of the wall
    D. formwork for one face of the wall, place the reinforcing steel for one face, place the form-work for the other face of the wall, then place the reinforcing steel for the second face

20. To obtain information concerning the product of a particular major manufacturer of flooring, the BEST of the following sources of information is the 20.____
    A. Architectural Standards   B. ASTM
    C. Sweet's Catalogue   D. Flooring Institute

21. Of the following, loose lintels would MOST likely be found in the specifications under the item entitled 21.____
    A. Ornamental Iron   B. Miscellaneous Iron
    C. Structural Steel   D. Hollow Metal Work

22. Galvanized metal lath is metal lath coated with 22.____
    A. tin   B. copper   C. zinc   D. nickel

23. In the welding symbol the 2 represents the 23.____
    A. spacing between welds in inches
    B. length of the weld in inches
    C. number of sides to be welded
    D. thickness of the throat of the weld in inches

24. The specification for a building states that rib lath should be 3.4 pounds. This MEANS 3.4 pounds per

    A. square foot
    B. linear foot of a 3 foot roll
    C. square yard
    D. 10 square feet

25. Terrazzo floors are laid with brass dividing strips PRIMARILY for the purpose of

    A. preventing slipping
    B. appearance
    C. preventing irregular cracking
    D. easy screeding

26. The PURPOSE of a chase is to

    A. support stair stringers
    B. accomodate pipes in a wall
    C. accomodate flashing in a parapet
    D. provide venting

27. In masonry work, a bull nose brick would be located at

    A. an inside corner
    B. an outside corner
    C. the key of an arch
    D. the roof of a boiler setting

28. The addition of lime to cement mortar improves the workability of mortar and

    A. increases the strength
    B. decreases the shrinkage
    C. decreases the weight
    D. increases the watertightness

29. Brickwork must be cleaned after completion of setting by

    A. scrubbing with soap solution and water
    B. wire brushing
    C. washing with muriatic solution
    D. sand blasting

30. In a multi-story building, weep holes in cavity wall brick construction are USUALLY placed in the brickwork

    A. above all masonry openings
    B. at foundation level only
    C. at the parapet only
    D. at every floor

31. A brick wall which consists of all stretcher courses is said to be built with a _____ Bond.

    A. Flemish
    B. Running
    C. English
    D. Common

32. The whitish deposit frequently seen on brick walls can USUALLY be avoided by

    A. using brick that contains more soluable salts
    B. keeping the water-mortar ratio high
    C. adding muriatic acid to the mortar
    D. constructing properly filled weathertight joints

33. Specifications for a building require brick to be wet before using.
    Of the following, the BEST reason for this requirement is that wetting

    A. makes it easier to place brick
    B. cleans the brick
    C. prevents absorption of moisture from the mortar
    D. shows up flaws in the brick that would otherwise be hidden

34. In checking the ingredients that are to go into the concrete for a footing that is being poured, you notice that there is 5% too much cement.
    Of the following, the BEST action to take in this situation is to

    A. do nothing
    B. condemn the footing
    C. increase the amount of sand in the mix
    D. order core borings taken of the finished footing

35. The soil conditions for a new building are MOST frequently checked by

    A. augering   B. soundings
    C. rodding   D. borings

KEY (CORRECT ANSWERS)

1.	B	16.	D
2.	C	17.	A
3.	D	18.	D
4.	C	19.	B
5.	B	20.	C
6.	D	21.	B
7.	B	22.	C
8.	B	23.	B
9.	B	24.	C
10.	B	25.	C
11.	C	26.	B
12.	C	27.	B
13.	A	28.	B
14.	C	29.	C
15.	D	30.	D

31. B
32. D
33. C
34. A
35. D

EXAMINATION SECTION
TEST 1

DIRECTIONS: Each question or incomplete statement is followed by several suggested answers or completions. Select the one that BEST answers the question or completes the statement. *PRINT THE LETTER OF THE CORRECT ANSWER IN THE SPACE AT THE RIGHT.*

1. Concrete with a slump of 2 inches would *most likely* be used for

    A. floors
    B. thin wall sections
    C. columns
    D. deep beams

2. The structure above the roof of a building which encloses a stairway is called a

    A. scuttle
    B. bulkhead
    C. penthouse
    D. shaft

3. A #4 reinforcing bar has a diameter, in inches, of *approximately*

    A. 1/4   B. 3/8   C. 1/2   D. 5/8

4. A spandrel beam will usually be found

    A. at the wall
    B. around stairs
    C. at the peak of a roof
    D. underneath a column

5. Oil is applied to the inside surfaces of concrete forms to

    A. prevent loss of water from the concrete
    B. obtain smoother concrete surfaces
    C. make stripping easier
    D. prevent honeycombing

6. A retaining wall is built with a batter.
   Of the following conditions, the one which *most likely* applies to the wall is

    A. it is out of plumb
    B. it is thinner at top than at bottom
    C. neither surface is vertical
    D. both surfaces are vertical

7. Two cubic yards of sand and four cubic yards of broken stone are to be used to make 1:2:4 concrete.
   If all the aggregate is used, the number of bags of cement that would be required is

    A. 1   B. 9   C. 18   D. 27

8. A rectangular plot is 30 feet wide by 60 feet long. The length of the diagonal, in feet, is *most nearly*

    A. 68   B. 67   C. 66   D. 65

9. Wood floor joists are supported on masonry walls which have a clear spacing of 17'0". The number of rows of cross-bridging required is

    A. 4   B. 3   C. 2   D. 1

10. When painting wood, the puttying of nail holes and cracks should be done 10.____

    A. *after* the priming coat is dry
    B. *before* the priming coat is applied
    C. *while* the priming coat is still wet
    D. *after* the finish coat is applied

11. The material that would normally be used to make a corbel in a brick wall is 11.____

    A. brick   B. wood   C. steel   D. concrete

12. Headers and trimmers are used in the construction of 12.____

    A. footings   B. walls   C. floors   D. arches

13. In the design of stairs, the designer should consider 13.____

    A. maximum height of riser only
    B. minimum width of tread only
    C. product of riser height by tread width only
    D. all of the above

14. A reduction in the required number of columns in a building can be made by using one of the following types of beam. Which one? 14.____

    A. floor   B. girder   C. cantilever   D. jack

15. Doors sheathed in metal are known as _____ doors. 15.____

    A. kalamein   B. tin-clad   C. bethlehem   D. flemish

16. A coat of plaster which is scratched deliberately would *most likely* be 16.____

    A. used in two-coat work only
    B. the first coat placed
    C. the second coat placed
    D. condemned by the inspector

17. A concealed draft opening is 17.____

    A. *good* because it improves the appearance of a room
    B. *bad* because it might be accidentally blocked up
    C. *good* because it can be used to regulate the flow of fresh air
    D. *bad* because it is a fire hazard

18. A groove is cut in the underside of a stone sill. This is done to 18.____

    A. keep rain water from running down the wall
    B. allow the insertion of dowels
    C. improve the mortar bond
    D. reduce the weight of the sill

19. Of the following, the one which would LEAST likely be used in conjunction with the others is

    A. rafter
    B. collar beam
    C. ridgeboard
    D. tail beam

20. The dimensions of a 2 x 4 when dressed are, *most nearly*,

    A. 2 x 4
    B. 1 1/2 x 3 1/2
    C. 1 5/8 x 3 5/8
    D. 1 3/4 x 3 1/2

21. The story heights of a building could be MOST readily determined from

    A. a plan view
    B. an elevation view
    C. a plot map
    D. all of the above

22. Honeycombing in concrete is *most likely* to occur

    A. if the forms are vibrated
    B. near the top of the forms
    C. if the mix is stiff
    D. if the concrete is well-spaded

23. A weather joint in brick work is one in which the mortar is

    A. flush with the face of the lower brick and slopes inward
    B. flush with the face of the upper brick and slopes inward
    C. recessed a fixed distance behind the face of the brick
    D. flush with the face of upper and lower brick but curves inward between the two bricks

24. A 12 inch brick wall is constructed using stretchers only.
    The PRINCIPAL objection to such a wall is with

    A. appearance
    B. construction difficulties
    C. bond
    D. dimensional problems

25. To prevent sagging joists from damaging a brick wall in the event of a fire, it is BEST to

    A. anchor the joists firmly in the wall
    B. make a bevel cut on the end of the joists
    C. use bridal irons to support the joists
    D. box out the wall for the joists

26. Flashing would *most likely* be found in a

    A. footing   B. floor   C. ceiling   D. parapet

27. Vermiculite is used in plaster to

    A. reduce weight
    B. permit easier cleaning
    C. give architectural effects
    D. reduce the mixing water required

28. The volume in cubic feet of a room 8'6" wide by 10'6" long by 8'8" high is *most nearly* 28.___

    A. 770 B. 774 C. 778 D. 782

29. A slab of concrete is 2'0" by 3'0" by 8" thick. 29.___
    The weight of the slab is, in pounds, *most nearly*

    A. 450 B. 500 C. 550 D. 600

30. Wainscoting is USUALLY found on 30.___

    A. floors B. walls C. ceilings D. roofs

31. A piece of wood covering the plaster below the stool of a window is called a(n) 31.___

    A. apron B. sill C. coping D. trimmer

32. English bond is used in 32.___

    A. plastering B. papering C. roofing D. bricklaying

33. In plastering, coves would *most likely* be found where 33.___

    A. wall meets ceiling B. one wall meets another
    C. wall meets floor D. wall meets column

34. Fire stopping is usually accomplished by 34.___

    A. installing self-closing doors
    B. bricking up the space between furring at floors
    C. installing wire glass
    D. using fire resistive materials throughout the building

35. A Class 1 (fireproof structure) building has floor sleepers of wood. This is 35.___

    A. *not permitted*
    B. *permitted*
    C. *permitted* if the space between sleepers is filled with incombustible material
    D. *permitted* if a wearing surface similar to asphalt tile is applied to the wooden flooring

KEY (CORRECT ANSWERS)

1.	A	16.	B
2.	B	17.	D
3.	C	18.	A
4.	A	19.	D
5.	C	20.	C
6.	B	21.	B
7.	D	22.	C
8.	B	23.	A
9.	C	24.	C
10.	A	25.	B
11.	A	26.	D
12.	C	27.	A
13.	D	28.	B
14.	C	29.	D
15.	A	30.	B

31. A
32. D
33. A
34. B
35. C

TEST 2

DIRECTIONS: Each question or incomplete statement is followed by several suggested answers or completions. Select the one that BEST answers the question or completes the statement. *PRINT THE LETTER OF THE CORRECT ANSWER IN THE SPACE AT THE RIGHT.*

1. Joints on interior surfaces of brick walls are usually flush joints EXCEPT when the walls are to be

    A. painted
    B. plastered
    C. waterproofed
    D. dampproofed

2. The headers in a brick veneer wall serve

    A. both a structural and an architectural purpose
    B. a structural purpose only
    C. an architectural purpose only
    D. NO structural or architectural purpose

3. Of the following, the one which is NOT usually classified as interior wood trim is

    A. apron   B. ribbon   C. jamb   D. base mold

4. Single-strength glass would *most likely* be found in

    A. single light sash
    B. doors in fire walls
    C. doors in fire partitions
    D. multi-light sash

5. The one of the following items that is LEAST related to the others is

    A. newel   B. riser   C. nosing   D. sill

6. In a plastered room, grounds for plaster are LEAST likely to be used

    A. at baseboards
    B. around windows
    C. around doors
    D. at the top of wainscoting

7. Of the following types of walls, the type which is *most likely* an interior wall is _____ wall.

    A. curtain   B. faced   C. panel   D. fire

8. *Boxing* is *most likely* to be performed by a

    A. mason
    B. plasterer
    C. plumber
    D. painter

9. Linseed oil is classified as a

    A. vehicle
    B. thinner
    C. drying oil
    D. pigment

10. Curing of concrete would be MOST critical when the temperature and humidity are, respectively,

    A. 75° and 80%
    B. 80° and 90%
    C. 85° and 10%
    D. 90° and 95%

11. Of the following items, the item which is LEAST related to the others is

    A. putty
    B. sash weight
    C. glazier's points
    D. lights

12. Assume that a wood-frame house has studs of 2 x 4's.
    Placing the studs so that the wider dimension is parallel to the wall is

    A. *good* because it provides a wider nailing surface for sheathing and lathing
    B. *bad* because it reduces the open space available for windows
    C. *good* because it stiffens the frame
    D. *bad* because it reduces the load-carrying capacity of the studs

13. Government anchors are used in one of the following types of construction. Which one?

    A. Wood frame
    B. Steel beams supported on masonry bearing walls
    C. Wooden joists on masonry bearing walls
    D. Steel frame with steel joists

14. When rivet holes in structural steel fail to match up by an eighth of an inch, the BEST thing to do is

    A. ignore the mismatch and force the rivet into the hole
    B. enlarge the holes with a drift pin
    C. ream the holes to a larger diameter
    D. use a smaller sized rivet

15. The BEST way to use two angles to make a lintel is

16. A single channel section would *most likely* be used for a

    A. floor beam
    B. girder
    C. spandrel beam
    D. column

17. An oil-base paint is usually thinned with

    A. linseed oil
    B. turpentine
    C. a drying oil
    D. a resin

18. Red lead is often used as a pigment in metal priming paints PRIMARILY because it

    A. provides good coverage
    B. presents a good appearance
    C. makes painting easier
    D. is a rust inhibitor

19. Knots in wood that is to be painted

   A. require no special treatment
   B. should be painted with the priming paint before the priming paint is applied to the rest of the wood
   C. should be coated with linseed oil before any painting is done
   D. should be coated with shellac before any painting is done

20. A dove-tail anchor would *most likely* be used to bond brick veneer with a _____ wall.

   A. brick   B. concrete   C. wood frame   D. concrete block

21. A rafter is MOST similar in function to a

   A. joist   B. stud   C. sill   D. girder

22. In steel construction, it is usually MOST important to mill the ends of

   A. beams   B. girders   C. columns   D. lintels

23. Furring tile is usually set so that the air spaces in the tile are

   A. continuous in a vertical direction
   B. continuous in a horizontal direction
   C. closed off at the ends of each tile
   D. set at random

24. When plastering a wall surface of glazed tile, it is MOST important that the tile

   A. be wet
   B. be dry
   C. be scored
   D. joints be raked

25. In a peaked roof, the run of a rafter is

   A. less than the length of the rafter
   B. greater than the length of the rafter
   C. equal to the length of the rafter
   D. dependent upon the slope of the rafter

26. Construction of a dormer window does NOT usually involve

   A. cut rafters
   B. rafter headers
   C. trimmer rafters
   D. hip rafters

27. In a four-ply slag roof,

   A. there is no overlap of the roofing felt
   B. a uniform coating of pitch or asphalt is placed on top of the top layer of felt
   C. slag is placed between the layers of felt
   D. there is no need to use flashing

28. Copper wire basket strainers would *most likely* be used by a

   A. carpenter   B. plumber   C. painter   D. roofer

4 (#2)

29. Splices of columns in steel construction are usually made 29.____

   A. at floor level
   B. two feet above floor level
   C. two feet below floor level
   D. midway between floors

30. In plumbing, a lead bend is usually used in the line from a 30.____

   A. slop sink   B. shower
   C. water closet   D. kitchen sink

31. The location of leaks in gas piping may be BEST detected by use of a 31.____

   A. match   B. heated filament
   C. soapy water solution   D. guinea pig

32. The one of the following items that would be MOST useful in eliminating water hammer from a water system is a 32.____

   A. magnesium anode   B. surge tank
   C. clean out   D. quick-closing valve

33. The MAIN purpose of a fixture trap is to 33.____

   A. catch small articles that may have accidentally dropped in the fixture
   B. prevent back syphonage
   C. make it easier to repair the fixture
   D. block the passage of foul air

34. In a certain district, the area of a building may be no longer than 55% of the area of the lot on which it stands. On a rectangular lot 75 ft. by 125 ft., the maximum permissible area of building is, in square feet, *most nearly* 34.____

   A. 5148   B. 5152   C. 5156   D. 5160

35. The allowable tensile stress in steel is 18,000 pounds per square inch. The maximum permissible tensile load in a 1-inch diameter steel bar is, in pounds, *most nearly* 35.____

   A. 13,500   B. 13,800   C. 14,100   D. 14,400

KEY (CORRECT ANSWERS)

1.	B	16.	C
2.	C	17.	B
3.	B	18.	D
4.	D	19.	D
5.	D	20.	B
6.	D	21.	A
7.	D	22.	C
8.	D	23.	B
9.	A	24.	C
10.	C	25.	A
11.	B	26.	D
12.	D	27.	B
13.	B	28.	D
14.	C	29.	B
15.	A	30.	C

31. C
32. B
33. D
34. C
35. C

TEST 3

DIRECTIONS: Each question or incomplete statement is followed by several suggested answers or completions. Select the one that BEST answers the question or completes the statement. *PRINT THE LETTER OF THE CORRECT ANSWER IN THE SPACE AT THE RIGHT.*

1. The ends of a joist in a brick building are cut to a bevel. This is done PRINCIPALLY to prevent damage to

   A. joist   B. floor   C. sill   D. wall

   1.____

2. Of the following, the wood that is MOST commonly used today for floor joists is

   A. long leaf yellow pine   B. douglas fir
   C. oak   D. birch

   2.____

3. Quarter sawed lumber is preferred for the best finished flooring PRINCIPALLY because it

   A. has the greatest strength
   B. shrinks the least
   C. is the easiest to nail
   D. is the easiest to handle

   3.____

4. Of the following, the MAXIMUM height that would be considered acceptable for a stair riser is

   A. 6 1/2"   B. 7 1/2"   C. 8 1/2"   D. 9 1/2"

   4.____

5. The part of a tree that will produce the DENSEST wood is the _____ wood.

   A. spring   B. summer   C. sap   D. heart

   5.____

6. Lumber in quantity is ordered by

   A. cubic feet   B. foot board measure
   C. lineal feet   D. weight and length

   6.____

7. A *chase* in a brick wall is a

   A. pilaster   B. waterstop   C. recess   D. corbel

   7.____

8. *Parging* refers to

   A. increasing the thickness of a brick wall
   B. plastering the back of face brickwork
   C. bonding face brick to backing blocks
   D. leveling each course of brick

   8.____

9. In brickwork, muriatic acid is commonly used to

   A. increase the strength of the mortar
   B. etch the brick
   C. waterproof the wall
   D. clean the wall

   9.____

10. Cement mortar can be made easier to work by the addition of a small quantity of

    A. lime   B. soda   C. litharge   D. plaster

11. Joints in brick walls are tooled

    A. immediately after each brick is laid
    B. after the mortar has had its initial set
    C. after the entire wall is completed
    D. 28 days after the wall has been built

12. If cement mortar has begun to set before it can be used in a wall, the BEST thing to do is to

    A. use the mortar immediately as is
    B. add a small quantity of lime
    C. add some water and mix thoroughly
    D. discard the mortar

13. The BEST flux to use when soldering galvanized iron is

    A. killed acid   B. sal-ammoniac
    C. muriatic acid   D. resin

14. The type of solder that would be used in *hard soldering* is _____ solder.

    A. bismuth   B. wiping   C. 50-50   D. silver

15. Roll roofing material is usually felt which has been impregnated with

    A. cement   B. mastic   C. tar   D. latex

16. The purpose of flashing on roofs is to

    A. secure roofing materials to the roof
    B. make it easier to lay the roofing
    C. prevent leaks through the roof
    D. insulate the roof from excessive heat

17. The type of chain used with sash weights is _____ link.

    A. flat   B. round
    C. figure-eight   D. basketweave

18. The material that would be used to seal around a window frame is

    A. oakum   B. litharge   C. grout   D. calking

19. The function of a window sill is *most nearly* the same as that of a

    A. jamb   B. coping   C. lintel   D. buck

20. Lightweight plaster would be made with

    A. sand   B. cinders   C. potash   D. vermiculite

21. The FIRST coat of plaster to be applied on a three-coat plaster job is the _____ coat.

    A. brown   B. scratch   C. white   D. keene

22. The FIRST coat of plaster over rock lath should be a _____ plaster. 22.____

 A. gypsum B. lime
 C. Portland cement D. pozzolan cement

23. The PRINCIPAL reason for covering a concrete sidewalk with straw or paper after the concrete has been poured is to 23.____

 A. prevent people from walking on the concrete while it is still wet
 B. impart a rough, non-slip surface to the concrete
 C. prevent excessive evaporation of water in the concrete
 D. shorten the length of time it would take for the concrete to harden

24. Concrete is *rubbed* with a(n) 24.____

 A. emery wheel B. carborundum brick
 C. sandstone D. alundum stick

25. To prevent concrete from sticking to forms, the forms should be painted with 25.____

 A. oil B. kerosene C. water D. lime

26. One method of measuring the consistency of a concrete mix is by means of a _____ test. 26.____

 A. penetration B. flow
 C. slump D. weight

27. A chemical that is sometimes used to prevent the freezing of concrete in cold weather is 27.____

 A. alum B. glycerine
 C. calcium chloride D. sodium nitrate

28. The one of the following that is LEAST commonly used for columns is 28.____

 A. wide flange beams B. angles
 C. concrete-filled pipe D. "I" beams

29. Fire protection of steel floor beams is MOST frequently accomplished by the use of 29.____

 A. gypsum block B. brick
 C. rock wool fill D. vermiculite gypsum plaster

30. A *Pittsburgh lock* is a(n) 30.____

 A. emergency door lock B. sheet metal joint
 C. elevator safety D. boiler valve

31. Of the following items, the one which is NOT used in making fastenings to masonry or plaster walls is a(n) 31.____

 A. lead shield B. expansion bolt
 C. rawl plug D. steel bushing

32. The term *bell and spigot* USUALLY refers to 32.____

 A. refrigerator motors B. cast iron pipes
 C. steam radiator outlets D. electrical receptacles

3 (#3)

33. In plumbing work, a valve which allows water to flow in one direction only is commonly known as a _____ valve.

   A. check   B. globe   C. gate   D. stop

34. A pipe coupling is BEST used to connect two pieces of pipe of

   A. the same diameter in a straight line
   B. the same diameter at right angles to each other
   C. different diameters at a 45° angle
   D. different diameters in a 1/8th bend

35. One method of testing fuses is to connect a pair of test lamps in the circuit in such a manner that the test lamp will light up if the fuse is good and will remain dark if the fuse is bad. In the illustration, 1 and 2 are fuses. In order to test if fuse 1 is bad, test lamps should be connected between

   A. A and B   B. B and D   C. A and D   D. C and B

36. Operating an incandescent electric light bulb at less than its rated voltage will result in

   A. shorter life and brighter light
   B. longer life and dimmer light
   C. brighter light and longer life
   D. dimmer light and shorter life

37. In order to control a lamp from two different positions, it is necessary to use

   A. two single pole switches
   B. one single pole switch and one four-way switch
   C. two three-way switches
   D. one single pole switch and one four-way switch

38. The PRINCIPAL reason for the grounding of electrical equipment and circuits is to

   A. prevent short circuits   B. insure safety from shock
   C. save power   D. increase voltage

39. The ordinary single-pole flush wall type switch must be connected

   A. across the line
   B. in the "hot" conductor
   C. in the grounded conductor
   D. in the white conductor

40. A strike plate is MOST closely associated with a

   A. lock   B. sash   C. butt   D. tie rod

41. A room is 7'6" wide by 9'0" long, with a ceiling height of 8'0". One gallon of flat paint will cover approximately 400 square feet of wall.
    The number of gallons of this paint required to paint the walls of this room, making no deductions for windows or doors, is *most nearly* _____ gallon.

    A. 1/4   B. 1/3   C. 3/4   D. 1

42. The cost of a certain job is broken down as follows:

    Materials $375
    Rental of equipment 120
    Labor   315

    The percentage of the total cost of the job that can be charged to materials is *most nearly*

    A. 40%   B. 42%   C. 44%   D. 46%

43. By trial, it is found that by using two cubic feet of sand, a 5 cubic foot batch of concrete is produced. Using the same proportions, the amount of sand required to produce 2 cubic yards of concrete is *most nearly* _____ cubic feet.

    A. 20   B. 22   C. 24   D. 26

44. It takes four men six days to do a certain job. Working at the same speed, the number of days it will take three men to do this job is

    A. 7   B. 8   C. 9   D. 10

45. The cost of rawl plugs is $2.75 per gross. The cost of 2,448 rawl plugs is

    A. $46.75   B. $47.25   C. $47.75   D. $48.25

KEY (CORRECT ANSWERS)

1. D	11. B	21. B	31. D	41. C
2. B	12. D	22. A	32. B	42. D
3. B	13. C	23. C	33. A	43. B
4. B	14. D	24. B	34. A	44. B
5. D	15. C	25. A	35. C	45. A
6. B	16. C	26. C	36. B	
7. C	17. A	27. C	37. C	
8. B	18. D	28. B	38. B	
9. D	19. B	29. D	39. B	
10. A	20. D	30. B	40. A	

EXAMINATION SECTION
TEST 1

DIRECTIONS: Each question or incomplete statement is followed by several suggested answers or completions. Select the one that BEST answers the question or completes the statement. *PRINT THE LETTER OF THE CORRECT ANSWER IN THE SPACE AT THE RIGHT.*

1. Assume that a two story building measures 21'6" x 53'7". It is in a district that calls for an open space ratio of .80. The required open space on this lot must be *most nearly* square feet.   1._____

    A. 922   B. 1152   C. 1843   D. 2880

2. Assume that the elevation at the back of a lot is 127.36 ft. and the elevation at the front of the same lot is 125.49 ft.   2._____
The difference in elevation between front and back of the lot is *most nearly*

    A. 1'10 1/8"   B. 1'10 1/4"   C. 1'10 3/8"   D. 1'10 1/2"

3. The sketch below represents the lowest story of a new building. In order for this story to be considered a basement, the elevation of the first floor must be AT LEAST   3._____

    A. 131.09   B. 131.14   C. 131.19   D. 131.24

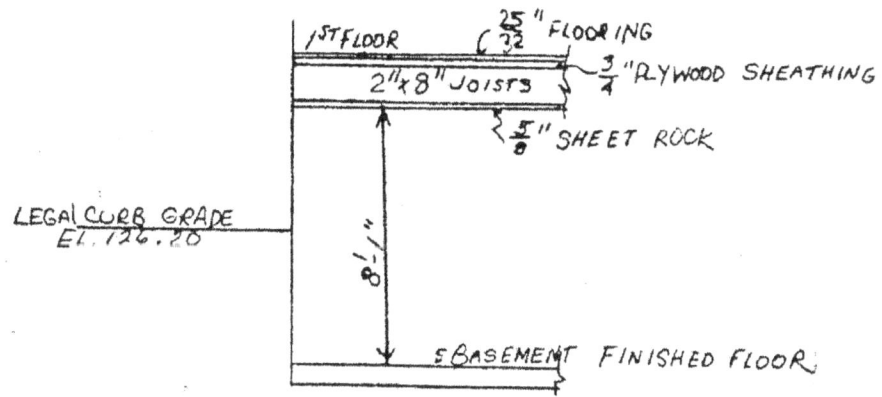

4. The MOST important requirement of a good report is that it should be   4._____

    A. properly addressed
    B. clear and concise
    C. verbose
    D. spelled correctly

5. Of the following, in determining whether a violation should be referred for court action, the MOST important item that should be considered is   5._____

    A. the amount of available time you have to process the case
    B. the availability of the inspector
    C. whether or not the owner has indicated a desire to cooperate with the department
    D. whether or not the case is important enough to warrant court action

6. In the Zoning Resolution, the size of required side yards would be found in the chapters on

   A. Use Groups
   B. Bulk Regulations
   C. Area Districts
   D. District Boundaries

7. According to the Zoning Resolution, the one of the following that is NOT considered part of the floor area of a building is a(n)

   A. basement
   B. stairwell at floor level
   C. penthouse
   D. attached garage on 1st floor

8. The one of the following that is permitted by the Zoning Resolution as a home occupation is

   A. veterinary medicine
   B. real estate broker
   C. teaching of music
   D. public relations agency

9. For the purpose of determining the number of rooms in a dwelling unit, the Zoning Resolution adds an arbitrary number to the number of *living rooms*.
   Where there are six or less living rooms, this arbitrary number is

   A. 1/2   B. 1   C. 1 1/2   D. 2

10. Assuming the following signs are all 10 square feet in area, the one that is NOT subject to the provisions of the Zoning Resolution is one indicating

    A. a freight entrance to a building
    B. a fund drive for a civic organization
    C. vacancies in an apartment building
    D. a parking area at the rear of a structure

11. On a plan, the symbol ~~~~~ represents

    A. earth
    B. wood
    C. metal lath
    D. marble

12. On a plan, the symbol represents

    A. cinder
    B. brick
    C. plywood
    D. rock lath and plaster

13. On a plan, the symbol represents

    A. glass
    B. asphalt shingles
    C. concrete
    D. porcelain enamel

14. A corbel is a form of

    A. cricket
    B. crown molding
    C. cantilever
    D. curtain wall

15. In balloon type framing, the second floor joists rest on a

    A. sole plate
    B. ribband
    C. header
    D. sill

16. Condensation of moisture in inadequately ventilated attics or roof spaces is usually GREATEST in

    A. summer   B. autumn   C. winter   D. spring

17. Of the following combinations of tread and riser, the one that would be acceptable for required stairs in either a new office building or a multiple dwelling is

    A. 9 1/4", 7 1/2"
    B. 9 1/2", 7 1/4"
    C. 9 1/2", 7 3/4"
    D. 10", 8"

18. A meeting rail is a common part of a

    A. door frame
    B. window sash
    C. stairwell
    D. bulkhead

19. If doors in an old building do not close, it is MOST probably an indication that the

    A. frames have shrunk
    B. building has settled
    C. hinges were not set properly
    D. wood used for the doors are of inferior grade

20. Cracks in concrete are not necessarily caused by settlement of a structure. Sometimes they are caused by

    A. shrinkage
    B. curing
    C. hydration
    D. over-troweling

KEY (CORRECT ANSWERS)

1. C
2. D
3. A
4. B
5. C

6. B
7. D
8. C
9. C
10. B

11. A
12. B
13. A
14. C
15. B

16. C
17. C
18. B
19. B
20. A

TEST 2

DIRECTIONS: Each question or incomplete statement is followed by several suggested answers or completions. Select the one that BEST answers the question or completes the statement. *PRINT THE LETTER OF THE CORRECT ANSWER IN THE SPACE AT THE RIGHT.*

1. Required exit doors from a room must open in the direction of egress when the room is occupied by more than _____ persons. 1._____

    A. 15   B. 25   C. 35   D. 50

2. A window in a masonry wall on a lot line 2._____

    A. is not permitted
    B. must have a fire resistive rating of 3/4 hour
    C. must have a fire resistive rating of 1 hour
    D. must have a fire resistive rating of 1 1/2 hours

3. Air entrained concrete is required in all cases for 3._____

    A. garage floors   B. footings
    C. grade beams   D. columns

4. A parapet wall or railing would be required on new non-residential structures where the height of the structure is greater than (give lowest height specified by law) _____ feet. 4._____

    A. 15   B. 19   C. 22   D. 25

5. Of the following statements, the one that is CORRECT is that wood joists may 5._____

    A. not be supported on a fire wall
    B. be supported on a fire wall only if fireproofed wall is used
    C. be supported on a fire wall only if they are separated from each other by at least 4 inches of solid masonry
    D. be supported on a fire wall only if they are separated from each other by at least 12 inches of solid masonry

6. A foundation wall below grade may be of hollow block only if the building 6._____

    A. is a residence
    B. is no more than one story high
    C. is of frame construction
    D. has no cellar or basement

7. The Building Code specifies that lintels are required to be fire-proofed when the opening is more than _____ feet. 7._____

    A. 3   B. 4   C. 5   D. 6

8. In a 12-inch brick wall, the MAXIMUM permitted depth of a chase is 8._____

    A. none   B. 4"   C. 6"   D. 8"

9. Wood joists should clear flues and chimneys by at least 9._____

    A. 1"   B. 2"   C. 3"   D. 4"

41

10. Fire retarding or enclosure in shafts of all vent ducts are required when they

    A. go through more than one floor
    B. are used for intake as well as exhaust
    C. are more than 144 square inches in area
    D. are in rooms subdivided with wood partitions

11. Assume a builder is unable to complete the pour for a continuous concrete floor slab. The slab is supported by beams and girders.
    The construction joint should be made at a point

    A. over a beam
    B. one quarter of the span length from the beam
    C. one third of the span length from the beam
    D. midway between beams

12. Under required stairs in a Class 3 building,

    A. it is unlawful to locate a closet
    B. a closet is permitted provided that the stringers are fire retarded
    C. a closet is permitted provided that the closet is completely lined with incombustible material
    D. a closet is permitted provided that fireproof wood is used to frame out the closet

13. In New York City, the exit provisions of the State Labor Law apply

    A. only to factories
    B. to factories and warehouses
    C. to factories, warehouses, and restaurants
    D. to all types of uses

14. A Class 3 building, two stories high, may have required stairs enclosed with stud partitions fire retarded with gypsum boards unless the building is used for a

    A. factory
    B. storage warehouse
    C. bowling alley
    D. department store

15. The one of the following rooms in a *place of assembly* that is required to be sprinklered is a

    A. performer's dressing room
    B. kitchen
    C. service pantry
    D. waiting room

16. Of the following, the FIRST operation in the demolition of a building is the

    A. shoring of the adjoining buildings
    B. erection of railings around stairwells
    C. removal of windows
    D. venting of the roof

17. As used in the Building Code, *consistency* of concrete refers to

    A. composition
    B. water-cement ratio
    C. relative plasticity
    D. proportion of aggregates

18. One condition that is required for a building to be considered a *Special Occupancy Structure* is that the building is used for

    A. a theater
    B. a church
    C. a restaurant
    D. motor vehicle repairs

19. A wire glass vision panel on a door opening into a fire tower is

    A. not permitted
    B. permitted if the panel has a fire rating of 3/4 hour
    C. permitted if the panel has a fire rating of 3/4 hour and is less than 100 square inches in area
    D. permitted if the panel has a fire rating of 3/4 hour, is less than 100 square inches in area, and is glazed with two thicknesses of wire glass with an air space between

20. One of the requirements that must be met before untreated wood can be used as a subdividing partition in a Class 1 building is that the partition

    A. be no more than 8 feet high
    B. enclose an area less than 200 square feet in size
    C. enclose office space only
    D. be made of a single thickness of wood

KEY (CORRECT ANSWERS)

1.	D	11.	D
2.	B	12.	C
3.	A	13.	A
4.	C	14.	C
5.	C	15.	A
6.	D	16.	C
7.	B	17.	C
8.	B	18.	A
9.	D	19.	A
10.	A	20.	D

TEST 3

DIRECTIONS: Each question or incomplete statement is followed by several suggested answers or completions. Select the one that BEST answers the question or completes the statement. *PRINT THE LETTER OF THE CORRECT ANSWER IN THE SPACE AT THE RIGHT.*

1. There are two criteria required for determining whether a multiple dwelling shall be classified as a *converted dwelling*.
   The FIRST is the number of families originally occupying the dwelling, and the second is the

   A. conjunctive uses
   B. date of erection of the building
   C. classification, whether Class A or B
   D. number of families now occupying the dwelling

   1.____

2. According to the Multiple Dwelling Law, a *dinette* is NOT considered a living room if its area is _____ sq. ft. or less.

   A. 50 B. 55 C. 59 D. 64

   2.____

3. Where a building faces only one street, the curb level used for measuring the height of the building is the

   A. lowest curb level in front of the building
   B. highest curb level in front of the building
   C. level of the curb at the center of the front of the building
   D. average of the levels of the lowest and highest curb level in front of the building

   3.____

4. According to the Multiple Dwelling Code, one of the living rooms in each apartment of a newly created multiple dwelling shall have a MINIMUM floor area of _____ square feet.

   A. 59 B. 110 C. 150 D. 175

   4.____

5. It is proposed to alter an old law tenement so as to increase the number of apartments. Of the following, the one that MOST completely gives the requirements to be met before the alteration can be approved is: Each new apartment must be provided a

   A. water closet
   B. water closet and a wash basin
   C. water closet, a wash basin, and a bath or shower
   D. water closet, a wash basin, a bath or shower, and centrally supplied heat

   5.____

6. Gas fueled space heaters may be permitted in lieu of centrally supplied heat.
   One of the following conditions required before the use of space heaters can be permitted is that

   A. each apartment has no more than two living rooms
   B. the building is a Class A multiple dwelling
   C. all apartments are used for single room occupancy
   D. D, the gas line supplying the heater be connected directly to the main so that the tenant cannot control the flow of gas

   6.____

7. An incinerator is required in all multiple

   A. dwellings
   B. dwellings four or more stories in height
   C. dwellings four or more stories in height and occupied by more than twelve families
   D. dwellings four or more stories in height occupied by more than twelve families and erected after October 1, 1951

8. Tests of required sprinkler systems in a single room occupancy building must be made

   A. monthly
   B. quarterly
   C. semi-annually
   D. annually

9. An additional apartment may be created on the first floor of a Class A frame converted dwelling provided that no more than two families will occupy this floor and

   A. the entrance hall is sprinklered
   B. the building is brick veneered
   C. there is no basement occupancy
   D. all stairs are enclosed in one hour fire partitions

10. The MAIN feature differentiating a *five tower* from a *fire stair* is the

    A. fire rating of the enclosure walls
    B. use to which the fire tower is put
    C. method of entering the fire tower from the building
    D. height of the fire tower

11. A new elevator shaft is to be built into a non-fireproof multiple dwelling.
    Of the following materials, the one that has the lowest fire resistance that would be acceptable for the enclosure walls of this shaft is

    A. 3" solid gypsum block
    B. 2" x 4" studs with 5/8" fire code 60 each side
    C. steel studs, wire mesh and 3/4" P.C. plaster
    D. 4" hollow concrete blocks, plastered both sides

12. Of the following statements, the one that is MOST complete and accurate is that a frame extension 70 sq. ft. in area added to a frame multiple dwelling is

    A. not permitted
    B. permitted only if the walls of the extension are brick filled
    C. permitted only if the walls of the extension are brick filled and the extension is to be used solely for bathrooms
    D. permitted only if the walls of the extension are brick filled, the extension is to be used solely for bathrooms and the walls are at least 3 ft. from the side lot lines

13. Assume it is proposed to extend a business use in a non-fireproof multiple dwelling by erecting an extension at the rear of the building.
    The roof the extension is required to be fireproof

    A. in all cases
    B. when the business use requires a combustible occupancy permit
    C. when there are fire escapes above the extension
    D. if the business use is a factory

14. In a Class A dwelling, two water closets may

    A. be placed in one compartment only in old law tenements
    B. be placed in one compartment in either old law or new law tenements
    C. be placed in one compartment in all types of apartment houses
    D. not be placed in one compartment

15. According to the Multiple Dwelling Law, a janitor is NOT required when the maximum number of families occupying the dwelling is

    A. 6　　　　B. 9　　　　C. 12　　　　D. 15

16. The first floor above the lowest cellar in a non-fireproof multiple dwelling does NOT have to be fireproof if

    A. the cellar is used only for incombustible storage
    B. there are two means of egress from the cellar
    C. the building is no more than three stories in height
    D. the dwelling is occupied by no more than nine families

17. In a converted multiple dwelling, ventilation of a room on the top story may be obtained by

    A. a skylight
    B. a duct with a wind blown hood
    C. a duct with an electrically operated fan
    D. by a window only and no other method is acceptable

18. *It* is proposed to build a closet under the stairs leading to the second floor in a non-fireproof *new law* tenement. This is

    A. not permitted
    B. permitted only if the entire closet is built of non-combustible materials
    C. permitted only if the closet is used for non-combustible storage
    D. permitted if the closet is built of fire-retarded partitions and the soffit of the stairs is also fire-retarded

19. For multiple dwellings erected after April 18, 1929, a ladder from a fire escape to a roof is NOT required when

    A. the building is three stories or less in height
    B. the roof is built of incombustible material
    C. the fire escape is on the front of the building
    D. there is no safe access from the roof to another building

20. It is proposed to convert a Class B multiple dwelling used for summer resort occupancy to year-round Class B use. This conversion is

    A. illegal
    B. legal provided the exits comply with the requirements for Class B use
    C. legal provided the exits and toilet facilities comply with the requirements for Class B use
    D. legal provided the exits, toilet facilities, and ventilation requirements comply with the requirements for Class B use

KEY (CORRECT ANSWERS)

1.	B	11.	A
2.	B	12.	A
3.	C	13.	C
4.	C	14.	A
5.	D	15.	C
6.	B	16.	C
7.	D	17.	A
8.	D	18.	A
9.	B	19.	C
10.	C	20.	A

EXAMINATION SECTION

DIRECTIONS: Each question or incomplete statement is followed by several suggested answers or completions. Select the one that BEST answers the question or or completes the statement. *PRINT THE LETTER OF THE CORRECT ANSWER IN THE SPACE AT THE RIGHT.*

1. A lintel is MOST CLOSELY associated with a
   A. wall opening
   B. floor opening
   C. roof opening
   D. fire escape

   1._____

2. An apron is MOST CLOSELY associated with a
   A. door
   B. window
   C. yard
   D. bulkhead

   2._____

3. In remodeling a multiple dwelling, brickwork has been removed from an interior steel column and replaced with 3/4" plaster. The MOST SERIOUS consequence of this alteration relates to
   A. strength
   B. corrosion
   C. fire
   D. accidental damage

   3._____

4. In multiple dwellings, hand-rails must be provided on each side of a stairway if the stairway exceeds CERTAIN
   A. height
   B. width
   C. steepness
   D. tread-riser ratio

   4._____

5. A rectangular court is 16'0" wide by 20'0" long. The length of a diagonal is, in feet, most nearly,
   A. 25.2
   B. 25.4
   C. 25.6
   D. 25.8

   5._____

6. If concrete weighs 4000 pounds per cubic yard, the weight of a slab of concrete 2'6" by 6'9" by 3'2" is, in pounds, most nearly,
   A. 7920
   B. 7830
   C. 7740
   D. 7650

   6._____

7. In the case of new construction, a certificate of occupancy is required for
   A. class A multiple dwellings
   B. class A and class B multiple dwellings
   C. all dwellings
   D. all buildings

   7._____

8. A sewer which carries BOTH sewage and storm water is known as a _____ sewer.
   A. sanitary
   B. combined
   C. separate
   D. storm

   8._____

9. A fire-restrictive rating of an assembly indicates that the assembly
   A. is incombustible
   B. is non-flammable
   C. can withstand a fire of given duration without serious failure
   D. prevents the passage of heat

   9._____

10. Major classifications of districts established by the Zoning Resolution do NOT Include _____ districts.
    A. Use   B. Height   C. Residence   D. Area

11. The distinction between a Business District and a Business-1 District relates to
    A. types of businesses
    B. size of businesses
    C. types of business signs
    D. area allowed for manufacturing

12. The MAXIMUM hight to which a multiple dwelling fronting on a 100-foot street may be erected in a class one and on-half district is
    A. 178 ft.   B. 175 ft.   C. 150 ft.   D. 125 ft.

13. As a senior supervisor of Housing, you are directed to interview several men whom the department is considering for provisional employment as a supervisor of Housing. During the course of your interview with one of these men, you learn that he has good building construction experience, owns his home outright in the City for the past four years, and even owns the patent rights on certain items now being used in building construction work. With respect to this man, you should recommend that he
    A. be employed for a trial period of 30 days
    B. be employed for a provisional period of 90 days
    C. should not be employed unless further questioning shows that he complies with the Residence Law
    D. should not be employed unless he divests himself of certain properties

14. Multiple dwellings of non-fireproof construction may NOT exceed
    A. 75 feet in height
    B. 6 stories in height unless provided with elevators
    C. 5 stories in height
    D. 60 feet in height

15. Construction in a non-fireproof multiple dwelling more than three stories high must be fireproof in all of the following locations EXCEPT
    A. first floor
    B. stairs
    C. elevator shaft below first floor
    D. roof

16. Flue or chimney connections for every apartment are MOST LIKELY to be required in
    A. tenements
    B. class A multiple dwellings
    C. class B multiple dwellings
    D. buildings used for single-room occupancy

17. In a 6-story multiple dwelling, the required access to the yard form a street may NOT be provided by a
    A. court
    B. fire proof passage
    C. fire-retarded passage
    D. direct passage 3'6" clear width by 7'0" high

18. The required area a function of the of windows in a living room is 18._____
    A. floor area
    B. room volume
    C. wall area
    D. number of occupants

19. A living room in a class A multiple dwelling is 8'0" wide by 9'6" long by 8'6" high. 19._____
    This room fails to meet requirements of the Multiple Dwelling Law with respect to
    A. height   B. volume
    C. area   D. least horizontal dimension

20. A tenant complains to an inspector that the interior lock on his dumbwaiter door is 20._____
    faulty and that the door is continually coming open. The inspector should, after
    verifying the facts,
    A. tell the tenant to notify the landlord
    B. notify the janitor and report a violation to the Department
    C. tell the tenant to fix it himself
    D. tell the janitor to fix this lock

21. Fire escapes constructed of material subject to rusting should be painted 21._____
    A. every year
    B. every two years
    C. whenever they become rusty
    D. twice a year

22. A building fronts on an unpaved street without curbs or sidewalk. The legal height 22._____
    of the building
    A. can not be established
    B. is established by the architect
    C. may be established from the equivalent curb level
    D. is established by the owner

23. The story heights of a class B multiple dwelling are as follows: cellar, 12 ft.; first floor, 23._____
    20 ft.; second floor, 15 ft.; third through sixth floors, 12 ft. The story height of the
    building is
    A. 6   B. 7   C. 8   D. 9

24. The distinction between "cellar" and "basement" is concerned with 24._____
    A. relative position with respect to curb elevation
    B. use
    C. height
    D. area

25. The distinction between fire-tower and fire-stair is based upon 25._____
    A. position with respect to building walls
    B. degree of fire-proofing
    C. height
    D. use of self-closing fireproof doors

26. Yards may NOT be omitted under any circumstances when a multiple dwelling occupies
    A. two or more entire blocks
    B. an interior lot
    C. an interior lot running through from street to street
    D. an entire block

27. A multiple dwelling is one which is occupied by at least
    A. 2 families   B. 3 families   C. 4 families   D. 5 familles

28. The distinction between class A and class B multiple dwellings relates to
    A. size   B. quality   C. fireproofing   D. residence

29. A portion of a multiple dwelling which is considered to be an apartment contains
    A. more than one room
    B. a kitchen
    C. a bathroom
    D. a water-closet compartment

30. Living rooms include
    A. water-closet compartments
    B. bathrooms
    C. kitchens
    D. foyers

31. Of the following, the one which is NOT considered to be an alteration is
    A. replacing wainscoting with plaster
    B. moving a building from one lot to another
    C. replacing bearing wall to make one large room from two small ones
    D. increasing the height of a building without increasing the number of stories

32. A trimmer arch is used in connection with a
    A. fireplace   B. window   C. closet door   D. stairway

33. A sidewalk shed
    A. is never permitted
    B. is used-when demolishing buildings
    C. is allowed in front of public buildings
    D. must have an open roof

Questions 34-39.
Questions 34 through 39 refer to the two columns below. Each item in Column 1 is associated with an item in Column 2. Place the letter of the item in Column 2 after the number of the item in Column 1 with which it is most closely associated. Items in Column 2 may be used more than once or not at all.

Column 1

34. Scratch coat
35. Flashing
36. Louvre
37. Bond
38. Soil stack
39. Shoring

Column 2

A. Welding
B. Bricklaying
C. Plumbing
D. Plastering
E. Roofing
F. Flooring
G. Excavating
H. Ventilatin

34._____
35._____
36._____
37._____
38._____
39._____

40. Of the following terms, the one which LEAST relates to the other is
    A. soffit   B. newel   C. nosing   D. trimmer

40._____

41. Of the following terms, the one which LEAST relates to the others is
    A. muntin   B. stop-bead   C. jamb   D. sill

41._____

42. Fire-stopping is synonymous with
    A. fireproofing
    C. fire-treated
    B. fire-retarding
    D. none of the foregoing

42._____

43. A two-story building 32'0" by 60'0" is erected on a lot 75'0" by 110'0". The floor area ratio is, most nearly,
    A. 0.46   B. 0.42   C. 0.38   D. 0.34

43._____

44. A portion of a multiple dwelling, other than an apartment or suite of rooms, separated as a unit from the rest of the building by fireproof construction, is known as a
    A. section   B. unit   C. separate   D. wing

44._____

45. Records maintained by the Department for each building in the City should include all of the following EXCEPT
    A. number of persons living in each apartment
    B. diagram of building
    C. date of erection
    D. deaths occurring in building each year

45._____

46. Hospitals are required to make a weekly report to the Department of cases of sickness received in such hospital. This report does NOT state
    A. patient's name
    B. patient's address
    C. patient's sickness
    D. whether patient is an adult or child

47. The Police Department is required to make a weekly report to the Department of arrests. The report does NOT contain
    A. name
    B. address
    C. offense
    D. disposition of case

48. Of the following City Departments, the one which must be furnished information by the Department is
    A. Hospitals
    B. Welfare
    C. Public Works
    D. Tax

49. In a new multiple dwelling, gas meters may be located in
    A. boiler rooms
    B. stair halls
    C. public halls above the cellar
    D. none of the foregoing

50. A required sink may be placed in a
    A. bathroom containing a water-closet
    B. water-closet compartment
    C. public hall
    D. none of the foregoing

(KEY (CORRECT ANSWERS)

1. A	11. C	21. C	31. A	41. C
2. B	12. A	22. C	32. A	42. D
3. C	13. D	23. C	33. B	43. A
4. B	14. A	24. A	34. D	44. A
5. C	15. D	25. A	35. E	45. A
6. A	16. A	26. B	36. H	46. A
7. D	17. C	27. B	37. B	47. D
8. B	18. A	28. D	38. C	48. D
9. C	19. C	29. C	39. G	49. D
10. C	20. B	30. C	40. D	50. D

EXAMINATION SECTION

TEST 1

DIRECTIONS: Each question or incomplete statement is followed by several suggested answers or completions. Select the one that BEST answers the question or completes the statement. *PRINT THE LETTER OF THE CORRECT ANSWER IN THE SPACE AT THE RIGHT.*

1. It is the policy of the department to hold each inspector responsible for formal work assignments given to him.
   Of the following, the BEST reason for this is that it
   A. enables division personnel to keep track of the work schedule
   B. encourages inspectors to be careful with written documents
   C. increases the speed with which inspections are carried out
   D. provides a double check on the time sheet records of inspectors

   1.____

2. Assume that you are faced with delays caused by absences of team members due to illness.
   Of the following, the BEST means of handling this problem is to
   A. have your team members keep an accurate record of their absences so that you will be able to identify anyone who is becoming accident-prone
   B. insist on prompt notification at all times when someone on your tea is absent because of illness
   C. require that your team members submit a memorandum informing you of the days on which they will be absent
   D. take over all tasks assigned to your team members when they are absent

   2.____

3. Assume that one of the men on your team tells you that he has a problem and would like to discuss it with you privately. During the course of this meeting, it becomes apparent that the man's difficulty stems from conflicts he is having with his wife.
   Of the following, the BEST course of action that you, his supervisor, should take in this situation is to
   A. advise the employee to meet with your superior, who might be able to give him more objective advice
   B. gather enough facts to advise the man about definite solutions for his problem
   C. help the man analyze what the problem is but leave the decision to him
   D. tell the man that you can talk to him only about problems that are job-related

   3.____

4. Sometimes it may be advantageous for a senior inspector to let the inspectors under his supervision participate in the development of decisions that must be made about the team's activities.
   The one of the following that is LEAST likely to result when team members participate in supervisory decisions is that the inspectors may

   4.____

A. be able to show leadership
B. have a chance to feel creative
C. require closer supervision
D. take more responsibility for minor problems

5. Of the following, the CHIEF reason that the senior inspector should take disciplinary measures as soon as possible after a subordinate inspector's violation of department rules is that
   A. delay will make the senior inspector seem lax
   B. the inspector is more likely to accept the discipline a justified
   C. the supervisor may forget about the offense
   D. there is less likelihood that other inspectors will find out about the offense

6. Assume that you have been directed to institute a new procedure for writing reports about violations encountered during the inspections conducted by the team of which you are in charge. You have heard, through the grapevine, that several of the experienced inspectors on the team have objections to this new procedure.
   Of the following, the BEST course of action for you to take FIRST in this situation is to
   A. issue a written order to put the new procedure into effect
   B. meet with all the inspectors on your team to discuss the procedure
   C. modify the procedure to make it acceptable to all of your inspectors
   D. postpone institution of the new procedure

7. Assume that the head of your unit expects to be out for a week because of illness. You are to act as head of the unit for that time.
   In determining what to do about those inspection duties that you were originally scheduled to perform and which should not be postponed, it would be MOST advisable to
   A. assign them to the inspector who needs training in this area
   B. assign them to the inspector with the most seniority
   C. attempt to do as many of them as possible yourself
   D. divide them among all inspectors who have the time and ability

8. The one of the following situations that is LEAST likely to result from poor planning and organization of an inspection unit's work is that
   A. inspectors will be uncertain about their responsibilities
   B. job performance will be poor
   C. the work will be completed at a steady monotonous pace
   D. there will be a high turnover rate in the unit's staff

9. Of the following, the BEST course of action to take in order to avoid charges of favoritism when making job assignments is to
   A. delegate the authority to make assignments to a well-liked experienced inspector
   B. keep records which may demonstrate proper distribution and rotation of assignments

C. select the oldest inspectors for the most desirable assignments
D. tell the men that, if they have any gripes about their assignments, they should see the supervising inspector

10. Of the following, the MOST important reason for a senior inspector to receive communications from the supervising inspector before they are transmitted to the inspectors is that he can
    A. avoid discussing communications with his subordinates
    B. exercises close supervision over every detail of the inspectors' assignments
    C. limit the amount of information received by his subordinates
    D. maintains his position in the chain of command

11. If an organization has rules that are clear but excessively detailed and rigid, the one of the following which is MOST likely to occur is that
    A. employees will tend to ignore the rules
    B. records of performance will be more difficult to maintain
    C. supervisors will have more difficulty in applying the rules to individual situations
    D. use of individual judgment and discretion will be decreased

12. An effective senior inspector strives to build up the feeling that he and his men are on the same team. The imposition of discipline may serious endanger the relationship built up between him and his men.
    The one of the following steps that the senior inspector may take to insure that the imposition of discipline will NOT cause any deterioration of his relationship with his subordinates is to
    A. avoid disciplinary action, except for very serious offenses
    B. delegate simple disciplinary problems to a competent, experienced inspector
    C. discipline his men in groups so that they will feel as if they were part of a team
    D. impose discipline in as impersonal way as possible

13. Suppose that one of the inspectors under the supervision of a senior inspector is repeatedly late for work. Despite the inspector's habitual lateness, he manages to complete his work assignments on schedule.
    Of the following, the MOST advisable action for the senior inspector to take in this situation is to
    A. ask one of the other inspectors to speak to him about his attendance
    B. ignore the inspector's habitual lateness as long as he does his work properly
    C. reprimand the inspector privately and follow through to see whether his attendance improves
    D. tell him in the presence of the other inspectors that he must improve his attendance record

14. Assume that you are informed by your superior that all reports prepared by your team should be checked by you when possible before their submission to a supervising inspector.
    Of the following, the BEST course of action to take if you are too busy to look at all these reports and they have to be sent out right away is to
    A. delegate the responsibility for checking the reports to someone you have carefully instructed in the need for neat and accurate reports
    B. request additional staff from another unit to help you review these reports
    C. send the reports out without checking them and attach an explanatory note, telling your superior that you have not had time to look at them
    D. tell our men to review one another's reports and initial them

15. Assume that a senior inspector notices that another senior inspector divides his team's workload in what seems to him to be an inefficient manner. He decides to report this to the supervising inspector.
    Of the following, an accurate evaluation of the action taken by the senior inspector in this situation is that it is GENERALLY
    A. *good* practice, mainly because the supervising inspector is the only person authorized to make this senior inspector divide the work according to standard procedure
    B. *good* practice, mainly because the senior inspector needs close supervision to adequately carry out his responsibilities
    C. *poor* practice, mainly because the senior inspector should have consulted other senior inspectors about this situation
    D. *poor* practice, mainly because the senior inspector should understand that other senior inspectors may manage their operations differently

16. Assume that you have heard a rumor that department rules are about to be changed in a manner which will make certain types of inspections more complicated.
    Of the following, the BEST action for you to take in this situation is to
    A. ask the members of your staff, individually, if they have heard such a rumor
    B. call a meeting of your staff to tell them such a change is rumored
    C. make plans to change your unit's procedures to adapt to the new methods
    D. await official confirmation or denial of the rumor

17. Assume that one of the inspectors under your supervision has been doing an excellent job but no longer seems to have any interest in the work. He complains to you that he finds the work boring.
    Of the following, the MOST advisable action for you to take FIRST is to
    A. ask some of his fellow inspectors to discuss the matter with him
    B. attempt to vary his assignments and give him more complex assignments
    C. remind him that his evaluation by superiors may depend in part on the interest he shows in his work
    D. suggest that the inspector be transferred to another division

18. The BEST way for you to prepare the inspectors in your unit to handle special assignments speedily and make decisions in an emergency is to
    A. follow each employee's work very carefully so you know where he is least efficient
    B. give them the freedom to make decisions in their everyday work
    C. refuse to accept work that is turned in late
    D. set deadlines ahead of the time when regularly assigned work is actually due so they will learn to work efficiently

19. Suppose you are supervising several inspectors. One of the inspectors has recently transferred to your unit. You discover that although he generally prepares his reports in a fairly correct way, he does not follow the prescribed procedure that you have taught the other inspectors.
    In this situation, the one of the following that it would be BEST for you to do is to
    A. allow him to use his own procedure if it is accurate and efficient
    B. refer him to your supervisor
    C. discuss the matter with all the inspectors and let them decide which procedure they wish to follow
    D. tell him to follow the procedure used by the other inspectors

20. Assume that you have one of your most competent inspectors working on a new type of project. As you are reviewing his work, you notice he has made some errors.
    You should
    A. correct the errors yourself, otherwise the inspector will get discouraged
    B. ignore the errors; they are probably not important, especially when the inspector is first learning the job
    C. tell the inspector about the errors; he will probably learn from them
    D. tell the inspector about the errors; then he will be aware that he is careless

21. Assume that your unit has been given a special assignment to make an original study. You plan to give this assignment to two of your most competent inspectors.
    The BEST way to start them on this work is to
    A. ask the two inspectors how they think the work can be done in a most effective way
    B. do some of the work with the inspectors to make sure they do not make any mistakes
    C. tell the inspectors they will be held directly responsible for the success of the study
    D. write up detailed instructions and give them to the inspectors who will do the work

22. Of the following steps in setting up an employee training program, the one which should PRECEDE the others is to
    A. assemble all the materials needed in the training program
    B. decide what training methods would be most effective
    C. determine what facilities are available for training purposes
    D. outline the areas that would be covered in the training program

23. Assume that you find it necessary to retrain an older, experienced inspector because you are giving this inspector a different kind of assignment.
    Of the following, the problem that is MOST likely to arise when retraining such a staff member is that the
    A. instructor will have disciplinary problems with this employee
    B. instructor will know less than this staff member
    C. employee at this status often lacks motivation to be retrained
    D. younger men will be unable to keep up with the performance of this employee

24. Assume that an inspector has recently been transferred from another unit and is now on your team.
    Of the following, the BEST method for you to use to determine whether this man needs any additional instruction or training is to
    A. ask him whether he is having difficulty with the work you assign to him
    B. ask the man's former supervisor whether he was a competent inspector
    C. review the way he handles the various tasks that you assign to him
    D. send this man into the field with one of your inspectors and have him evaluate the newly assigned inspector

25. Instituting a program of on-the-job training may sometimes present problems for the supervisor because, when first initiated, such training
    A. does not take place under actual working conditions
    B. is less instructive than formal training sessions
    C. may result in a decrease in the authority of the supervisor
    D. may slow down the unit's work

26. Suppose that you are approached by a newly appointed inspector who asks you to make an inspection visit with him because he is unsure of the procedure.
    The one of the following that you should do FIRST is to
    A. agree to make the visit with him
    B. refer him to the supervisor for help
    C. report him to the supervisor for incorrect behavior
    D. tell him to do the best he can and offer to help him write up the report

27. Suppose that you are writing up your inspection reports in your office on a particular day. A fellow inspector, who has left his identification at home, asks if he may use your identification card and badge in order to perform his scheduled inspections.

Of the following, you should
- A. allow him to use your identification since he is an inspector
- B. offer to perform the inspections for him if he will write the reports
- C. refuse his request and suggest he explain the situation to the supervisor
- D. tell him you need your identification for yourself

28. Assume that you are assigned to handle telephone complaints. After you have attempted to handle a complaint from a belligerent caller, the caller asks your name, saying that he is going to report you to your superior for being insolent to him.
It would be BEST for you to
- A. give the caller a false name so he will stop bothering you
- B. give the caller your name and explain the circumstances to your superior afterwards
- C. refuse to give the caller your name
- D. tell the caller that you have not been insolent to him

29. As a senior inspector, you are permitted to hold an outside job as long as it is NOT
- A. dangerous
- B. in conflict with the performance of your inspection duties
- C. mentally or physically taxing
- D. paid at a rate higher than your inspector job

30. Of the following, the MOST important reason that graphs and charts are used in reports to present material that can be treated statistically is that such material
- A. is easier to understand when it is presented in graph or chart form
- B. looks more impressive when it is presented in graph or chart form
- C. requires less time to prepare when it is presented in a graph or chart form instead of written out
- D. take up less space in graph or chart form than when it is written out

KEY (CORRECT ANSWERS)

1.	A	11.	D	21.	A
2.	B	12.	D	22.	D
3.	C	13.	C	23.	C
4.	C	14.	A	24.	C
5.	B	15.	D	25.	D
6.	B	16.	D	26.	B
7.	D	17.	B	27.	C
8.	C	18.	B	28.	B
9.	B	19.	D	29.	B
10.	D	20.	C	30.	A

TEST 2

DIRECTIONS: Each question or incomplete statement is followed by several suggested answers or completions. Select the one that BEST answers the question or completes the statement. *PRINT THE LETTER OF THE CORRECT ANSWER IN THE SPACE AT THE RIGHT.*

1. If an inspector finds a discrepancy between the plans and specifications, he should
   A. always follow the plans
   B. ask for an interpretation
   C. always follow the specifications
   D. follow the plans if the difference is in dimensions

   1.____

2. In performing field inspectional work, an inspector is the contact man between the public and the agency, and it is his job to secure compliance through the maximum utilization of persuasion and education and the minimum application of coercion.
   According to this statement, an inspector performing inspectional duties should
   A. seek to obtain voluntary compliance and use coercion only as a last resort
   B. be conciliatory on all issues of non-compliance and not take an attitude of firmness and authority
   C. maintain a strictly impersonal attitude in the exercise of his duties at all times
   D. use the threat of legal action to secure conformance with specified requirements

   2.____

3. The BEST way for a supervising inspector to determine whether a new inspector is learning his work properly is to
   A. ask the other men how this man is making out
   B. question him directly on details of the work
   C. assume that if he asks no questions, he knows the work
   D. inspect and follow up on the work which is assigned to him

   3.____

4. In assigning his men to various jobs, the BEST principle for a supervising inspector to follow is to
   A. study the men's abilities and assign them accordingly
   B. rotate a man from job to job until you find one which he can do well
   C. assign each of them to a job and let them adjust to it in their own way
   D. assume that men appointed to the position can do all parts of the work equally well

   4.____

5. Good inspection methods require that the inspector
   A. be observant and check all details
   B. constantly check with the engineer who designed the job
   C. apply specifications according to his interpretations
   D. permit slight job variation to establish good public relations

   5.____

6. An inspector inspecting a large job under construction inspected plumbing at 9 A.M., heating at 10 A.M., and ventilation at 11 A.M., and did his officework in the afternoon. He followed the same pattern daily for months.
   This procedure is
   A. *bad*, because not enough time is devoted to plumbing
   B. *bad*, because the tradesmen know when the inspections will occur
   C. *good*, because it is methodical and he does not miss any of the trades
   D. *good*, because it gives equal amount of time to the important trades

6.____

7. The BEST way to evaluate the overall state of completion of a construction project is to check the progress estimate against the
   A. inspection worksheet   B. construction schedule
   C. inspector's checklist   D. equipment maintenance schedule

7.____

8. When a contractor fails to adhere to an approved progress schedule, he should
   A. revise the schedule without delay
   B. ask for an extension of time on account of delays
   C. adopt such additional means and methods of construction as will make up for time lost
   D. take no immediate action with the hope that sufficient time will be available later on that will assure the completion in accordance with the schedule

8.____

9. The usual contract for agency work includes a section entitled instructions to bidders, which states that the
   A. contractor agrees that he has made his own examination and will make no claim for damages on account of errors or omissions
   B. contractor shall not make claims for damages of any discrepancy, error or omission in any plans
   C. estimates of quantities and calculations are guaranteed by the agency to be correct and are deemed to be a representation of the conditions affecting the work
   D. plans, measurement, dimensions, and conditions under which the work is to be performed are guaranteed by the agency

9.____

10. A lump sum type of contract may require the contractor to submit a schedule of unit price.
    The BEST reason for this is that it
    A. prevents the lump sum from being too high
    B. simplifies the selection of the lowest bidder
    C. enables the estimators to check the total cost
    D. provides a means of making equitable partial payments

10.____

11. A contractor on a large construction project USUALLY receives partial payments based on
    A. estimates of completed work
    B. actual cost of materials delivered and work completed
    C. estimates of material delivered and not paid for by the contractor
    D. the breakdown estimate submitted after the contract was signed and prorated over the estimated duration of the contract

    11._____

12. In order to avoid disputes over payments for extra work in a contract for construction, the BEST procedure to follow would be to
    A. have contractor submit work progress reports daily
    B. insert a special clause in the contract specifications
    C. have a representative on the job at all times to verify conditions
    D. allocate a certain percentage of the cost of the job to cover such expenses

    12._____

13. A fixed amount of money is generally withheld from the contractor for a definite period after the completion of construction.
    The BEST reason for this is
    A. that the money will be available for taxes due
    B. to penalize the contractor for poor work
    C. that it is a security for the repair of any defective work
    D. that the money will be available for modifications in the design of the structure

    13._____

14. Prior to the installation of equipment called for in the specifications, the contractor is USUALLY required to submit for approval
    A. sets of shop drawings
    B. a set of revised specifications
    C. a detailed description of the methods of work to be used
    D. a complete list of skilled and unskilled tradesmen he proposes to use

    14._____

15. During the actual construction work, the CHIEF value of a construction schedule is to
    A. insure that the work will be done on time
    B. reveal whether production is falling behind
    C. show how much equipment and material is required for the project
    D. furnish data as to the methods and techniques of construction operations

    15._____

16. Of the following items, the one which should NOT be included in a proposed work schedule is
    A. a schedule of hourly wage rates and supplementary benefits
    B. an estimated time required for delivery of materials and equipment
    C. the anticipated commencement and completion of the various operations
    D. the sequence and inter-relationship of various operations with those of related contracts

    16._____

17. The frequency with which job reports are submitted should depend MAINLY on   17.____
    A. how comprehensive the report has to be
    B. the amount of information in the report
    C. the availability of an experienced man to write the report
    D. the importance of changes in the information included in the report

18. The CHIEF purpose in preparing an outline for a report is usually to insure   18.____
    that
    A. the report will be grammatically correct
    B. every point will be given equal emphasis
    C. principal and secondary points will be properly integrated
    D. the language of the report will be of the same level and include the same technical terms

19. The MAIN reason for requiring written job reports is to   19.____
    A. avoid the necessity of oral orders
    B. develop better methods of doing the work
    C. provide a permanent record of what was done
    D. increase the amount of work that can be done

20. Assume you are recommending in a report to your superior that a radical   20.____
    change in a standard maintenance procedure should be adopted.
    Of the following, the MOST important information to be included in this report is
    A. a list of the reasons for making this change
    B. the names of others who favor the change
    C. a complete description of the present procedure
    D. amount of training time needed for the new procedure

KEY (CORRECT ANSWERS)

1.	B	11.	A
2.	A	12.	C
3.	B	13.	C
4.	A	14.	A
5.	A	15.	B
6.	B	16.	A
7.	B	17.	D
8.	C	18.	C
9.	A	19.	C
10.	D	20.	A

PREPARING WRITTEN MATERIAL
EXAMINATION SECTION
TEST 1

DIRECTIONS: Each of the sentences in this test may be classified under one of the following four categories:
  A. Faulty because of incorrect grammar or word usage
  B. Faulty because of incorrect punctuation
  C. Faulty because of incorrect capitalization or incorrect spelling
  D. Correct

Examine each sentence carefully to determine under which of the above four options it is best classified. Then, in the space to the right, print the capital letter preceding the option which is the BEST of the four suggested above. (Note that each faulty sentence contains but one type of error. Consider a sentence to be correct if it contains none of the types of errors mentioned, even though there may be other correct ways of expressing the same thought.)

1. He sent the notice to the clerk who you hired yesterday. 1.____

2. It must be admitted, however that you were not informed of this change. 2.____

3. Only the employee who have served in this grade for at least two years are eligible for promotion. 3.____

4. The work was divided equally between she and Mary. 4.____

5. He thought that you were not available at that time. 5.____

6. When the messenger returns; please give him this package. 6.____

7. The new secretary prepared, typed, addressed, and delivered, the notices. 7.____

8. Walking into the room, his desk can be seen at the rear. 8.____

9. Although John has worked here longer than She, he produces a smaller amount of work. 9.____

10. She said she could of typed this report yesterday. 10.____

11. Neither one of these procedures are adequate for the efficient performance of this task. 11.____

12. The typewriter is the tool of the typist; the cash register, the tool of the cashier. 12.____

2 (#1)

13. "The assignment must be completed as soon as possible" said the supervisor.   13._____

14. As you know, office handbooks are issued to all new Employees.   14._____

15. Writing a speech is sometimes easier than to deliver it before an audience.   15._____

16. Mr. Brown our accountant, will audit the accounts next week.   16._____

17. Give the assignment to whomever is able to do it most efficiently.   17._____

18. The supervisor expected either your or I to file these reports.   18._____

KEY (CORRECT ANSWERS)

1.	A	11.	A
2.	B	12.	C
3.	D	13.	B
4.	A	14.	C
5.	D	15.	A
6.	B	16.	B
7.	B	17.	A
8.	A	18.	A
9.	C		
10.	A		

TEST 2

DIRECTIONS: Each of the sentences in this test may be classified under one of the following four categories:
- A. Faulty because of incorrect grammar or word usage
- B. Faulty because of incorrect punctuation
- C. Faulty because of incorrect capitalization or incorrect spelling
- D. Correct

Examine each sentence carefully to determine under which of the above four options it is best classified. Then, in the space to the right, print the capital letter preceding the option which is the BEST of the four suggested above. (Note that each faulty sentence contains but one type of error. Consider a sentence to be correct if it contains none of the types of errors mentioned, even though there may be other correct ways of expressing the same thought.)

1. The fire apparently started in the storeroom, which is usually locked.   1._____
2. On approaching the victim, two bruises were noticed by this officer.   2._____
3. The officer, who was there examined the report with great care.   3._____
4. Each employee in the office had a seperate desk.   4._____
5. All employees including members of the clerical staff, were invited to the lecture. 5._____
6. The suggested Procedure is similar to the one now in use.   6._____
7. No one was more pleased with the new procedure than the chauffeur.   7._____
8. He tried to persaude her to change the procedure.   8._____
9. The total of the expenses charged to petty cash were high.   9._____
10. An understanding between him and I was finally reached.   10._____

KEY (CORRECT ANSWERS)

1.	D	6.	C
2.	A	7.	D
3.	B	8.	C
4.	C	9.	A
5.	B	10.	A

TEST 3

DIRECTIONS: Each of the sentences in this test may be classified under one of the following four categories:
- A. Faulty because of incorrect grammar or word usage
- B. Faulty because of incorrect punctuation
- C. Faulty because of incorrect capitalization or incorrect spelling
- D. Correct

Examine each sentence carefully to determine under which of the above four options it is best classified. Then, in the space to the right, print the capital letter preceding the option which is the BEST of the four suggested above. (Note that each faulty sentence contains but one type of error. Consider a sentence to be correct if it contains none of the types of errors mentioned, even though there may be other correct ways of expressing the same thought.)

1. They told both he and I that the prisoner had escaped. 1.____

2. Any superior officer, who, disregards the just complaint of his subordinates, is remiss in the performance of his duty. 2.____

3. Only those members of the national organization who resided in the Middle West attended the conference in Chicago. 3.____

4. We told him to give the national organization assignment to whoever was available. 4.____

5. Please do not disappoint and embarass us by not appearing in court. 5.____

6. Although the office's speech proved to be entertaining, the topic was not relevent to the main theme of the conference. 6.____

7. In February all new officers attended a training course in which they were learned in their principal duties and the fundamental operating procedure of the department. 7.____

8. I personally seen inmate Jones threaten inmates Smith and Green with bodily harm if they refused to participate in the plot. 8.____

9. To the layman, who on a chance visit to the prison observes everything functioning smoothly, the maintenance of prison discipline may seem to be a relatively easily realizable objective. 9.____

10. The prisoners in cell block fourty were forbidden to sit on the cell cots during the recreation hour. 10.____

KEY (CORRECT ANSWERS)

1. A   6. C
2. B   7. A
3. C   8. A
4. D   9. D
5. C   10. C

TEST 4

DIRECTIONS: Each of the sentences in this test may be classified under one of the following four categories:
- A. Faulty because of incorrect grammar or word usage
- B. Faulty because of incorrect punctuation
- C. Faulty because of incorrect capitalization or incorrect spelling
- D. Correct

Examine each sentence carefully to determine under which of the above four options it is best classified. Then, in the space to the right, print the capital letter preceding the option which is the BEST of the four suggested above. (Note that each faulty sentence contains but one type of error. Consider a sentence to be correct if it contains none of the types of errors mentioned, even though there may be other correct ways of expressing the same thought.)

1. I cannot encourage you any.   1.____
2. You always look well in those sort of clothes.   2.____
3. Shall we go to the park?   3.____
4. The man whome he introduced was Mr. Carey.   4.____
5. She saw the letter laying here this morning.   5.____
6. It should rain before the Afternoon is over.   6.____
7. They have already went home.   7.____
8. That Jackson will be elected is evident.   8.____
9. He does not hardly approve of us.   9.____
10. It was he, who won the prize.   10.____

KEY (CORRECT ANSWERS)

1.	A	6.	C
2.	A	7.	A
3.	D	8.	D
4.	C	9.	A
5.	A	10.	B

TEST 5

DIRECTIONS: Each of the sentences in this test may be classified under one of the following four categories:
  A. Faulty because of incorrect grammar or word usage
  B. Faulty because of incorrect punctuation
  C. Faulty because of incorrect capitalization or incorrect spelling
  D. Correct

Examine each sentence carefully to determine under which of the above four options it is best classified. Then, in the space to the right, print the capital letter preceding the option which is the BEST of the four suggested above. (Note that each faulty sentence contains but one type of error. Consider a sentence to be correct if it contains none of the types of errors mentioned, even though there may be other correct ways of expressing the same thought.)

1. Shall we go to the park.   1.____
2. They are, alike, in this particular way.   2.____
3. They gave the poor man sume food when he knocked on the door.   3.____
4. I regret the loss caused by the error.   4.____
5. The students' will have a new teacher.   5.____
6. They sweared to bring out all the facts.   6.____
7. He decided to open a branch store on 33rd street.   7.____
8. His speed is equal and more than that of a racehorse.   8.____
9. He felt very warm on that Summer day.   9.____
10. He was assisted by his friend, who lives in the next house.   10.____

KEY (CORRECT ANSWERS)

1.	B	6.	A
2.	B	7.	C
3.	C	8.	A
4.	D	9.	C
5.	B	10.	D

TEST 6

DIRECTIONS: Each of the sentences in this test may be classified under one of the following four categories:
- A. Faulty because of incorrect grammar or word usage
- B. Faulty because of incorrect punctuation
- C. Faulty because of incorrect capitalization or incorrect spelling
- D. Correct

Examine each sentence carefully to determine under which of the above four options it is best classified. Then, in the space to the right, print the capital letter preceding the option which is the BEST of the four suggested above. (Note that each faulty sentence contains but one type of error. Consider a sentence to be correct if it contains none of the types of errors mentioned, even though there may be other correct ways of expressing the same thought.)

1. The climate of New York is colder than California. 1.____
2. I shall wait for you on the corner. 2.____
3. Did we see the boy who, we think, is the leader. 3.____
4. Being a modest person, John seldom talks about his invention. 4.____
5. The gang is called the smith street bos. 5.____
6. He seen the man break into the store. 6.____
7. We expected to lay still there for quite a while. 7.____
8. He is considered to be the Leader of his organization. 8.____
9. Although I recieved an invitation, I won't go. 9.____
10. The letter must be here some place. 10.____

KEY (CORRECT ANSWERS)

1.	A	6.	A
2.	D	7.	A
3.	B	8.	C
4.	D	9.	C
5.	C	10.	A

TEST 7

DIRECTIONS: Each of the sentences in this test may be classified under one of the following four categories:
- A. Faulty because of incorrect grammar or word usage
- B. Faulty because of incorrect punctuation
- C. Faulty because of incorrect capitalization or incorrect spelling
- D. Correct

Examine each sentence carefully to determine under which of the above four options it is best classified. Then, in the space to the right, print the capital letter preceding the option which is the BEST of the four suggested above. (Note that each faulty sentence contains but one type of error. Consider a sentence to be correct if it contains none of the types of errors mentioned, even though there may be other correct ways of expressing the same thought.)

1. I though it to be he. 1.____
2. We expect to remain here for a long time. 2.____
3. The committee was agreed. 3.____
4. Two-thirds of the building are finished. 4.____
5. The water was froze. 5.____
6. Everyone of the salesmen must supply their own car. 6.____
7. Who is the author of Gone With the Wind? 7.____
8. He marched on and declaring that he would never surrender. 8.____
9. Who shall I say called? 9.____
10. Everyone has left but they. 10.____

KEY (CORRECT ANSWERS)

1.	A	6.	A
2.	D	7.	B
3.	D	8.	A
4.	A	9.	D
5.	A	10.	D

TEST 8

DIRECTIONS: Each of the sentences in this test may be classified under one of the following four categories:
- A. Faulty because of incorrect grammar or word usage
- B. Faulty because of incorrect punctuation
- C. Faulty because of incorrect capitalization or incorrect spelling
- D. Correct

Examine each sentence carefully to determine under which of the above four options it is best classified. Then, in the space to the right, print the capital letter preceding the option which is the BEST of the four suggested above. (Note that each faulty sentence contains but one type of error. Consider a sentence to be correct if it contains none of the types of errors mentioned, even though there may be other correct ways of expressing the same thought.)

1. Who did we give the order to?   1._____
2. Send your order in immediately.   2._____
3. I believe I paid the Bill.   3._____
4. I have not met but one person.   4._____
5. Why aren't Tom, and Fred, going to the dance?   5._____
6. What reason is there for him not going?   6._____
7. The seige of Malta was a tremendous event.   7._____
8. I was there yesterday I assure you   8._____
9. Your ukulele is better than mine.   9._____
10. No one was there only Mary.   10._____

KEY (CORRECT ANSWERS)

1.	A	6.	A
2.	D	7.	C
3.	C	8.	B
4.	A	9.	C
5.	B	10.	A

TEST 9

DIRECTIONS: In each of the following groups of sentences, one of the four sentences is faulty in grammar, punctuation, or capitalization. Select the INCORRECT sentence in each case.

1. A. If you had stood at home and done your homework, you would not have failed in arithmetic.
   B. Her affected manner annoyed every member of the audience.
   C. How will the new law affect our income taxes?
   D. The plants were not affected by the long, cold winter, but they succumbed to the drought of summer.

   1._____

2. A. He is one of the most able men who have been in the Senate.
   B. It is he who is to blame for the lamentable mistake.
   C. Haven't you a helpful suggestion to make at this time?
   D. The money was robbed from the blind man's cup.

   2._____

3. A. The amount of children in this school is steadily increasing.
   B. After taking an apple from the table, she went out to play.
   C. He borrowed a dollar from me.
   D. I had hoped my brother would arrive before me.

   3._____

4. A. Whom do you think I hear from every week?
   B. Who do you think is the right man for the job?
   C. Who do you think I found in the room?
   D. He is the man whom we considered a good candidate for the presidency.

   4._____

5. A. Quietly the puppy laid down before the fireplace.
   B. You have made your bed; now lie in it.
   C. I was badly sunburned because I had lain too long in the sun.
   D. I laid the doll on the bed and left the room.

   5._____

KEY (CORRECT ANSWERS)

1. A
2. D
3. A
4. C
5. A

READING COMPREHENSION
UNDERSTANDING AND INTERPRETING WRITTEN MATERIAL
EXAMINATION SECTION
TEST 1

DIRECTIONS: Each question or incomplete statement is followed by several suggested answers or completions. Select the one that BEST answers the question or completes the statement. *PRINT THE LETTER OF THE CORRECT ANSWER IN THE SPACE AT THE RIGHT.*

Questions 1-3.

DIRECTIONS: Questions 1 through 3 are to be answered SOLELY on the basis of the following paragraph.

The aging housing inventory presents a broad spectrum of conditions, from good upkeep to unbelievable deterioration. Buildings, even relatively good buildings, are likely to have numerous minor violations rather than the gross and evident sanitary violations of an earlier age. Except for the serious violations in a relatively small number of slum buildings, the task is to deal with masses of minor violations that, though insignificant in themselves, amount in the aggregate to major deprivations of health and comfort to tenants. Caused by wear and tear, by the abrasions of time, and aggravated by neglect, these conditions do not readily yield to the dramatic *vacate and restore* measures of earlier times. Moreover, the lines between *good* and *bad* housing have become blurred in many parts of our cities; we find a range of *shades of gray* blending into each other. Different kinds of code enforcement efforts may be required to deal with different degrees of deterioration.

1. The above passage suggests that code enforcement efforts may have to be   1.____

   A. developed to cope with varying levels of housing dilapidation
   B. aimed primarily at the serious violations in slum buildings
   C. modeled on the *vacate and restore* measures of earlier times
   D. modified to reduce unrealistic penalties for petty violations

2. According to the above passage, during former times some buildings had sanitary violations which were   2.____

   A. irreparable and minor
   B. blurred and gray
   C. flagrant and obvious
   D. insignificant and numerous

3. According to the above passage, the aging housing stock presents a   3.____

   A. great number of rent-controlled buildings
   B. serious problem of tenant-caused deterioration
   C. significant increase in buildings without intentional violations
   D. wide range of physical conditions

Questions 4-5.

DIRECTIONS: Questions 4 and 5 are to be answered SOLELY on the basis of the following passage.

In general, housing code provisions relating to the safe and sanitary maintenance of dwelling units prescribe the maintenance required for foundations, walls, ceilings, floors, windows, doors, stairways, and also the facilities and equipment required in other sections. The more recent codes have, in addition, extensive provisions designed to ensure that the unit be maintained in a rat-free and rat-proof condition. Also, as an example of new approaches in code provisions, one proposed Federal model housing code prohibits the landlord from terminating vital services and utilities except during temporary emergencies or when actual repairs or maintenance are in process. This provision may be used to prevent a landlord from turning off utility services as a technique of self-help eviction or as a weapon against rent strikes.

4. According to the above passage, the more recent housing codes have extensive provisions designed to 4.____

   A. maintain a reasonably fire-proof living unit
   B. prohibit tenants from participating in rent strikes
   C. maintain the unit free from rats
   D. prohibit tenants from using lead-based paints

5. According to the above passage, one housing code would permit landlords to terminate vital services during 5.____

   A. a rent strike
   B. an actual eviction
   C. a temporary emergency
   D. the planning of repairs and maintenance

Questions 6-8.

DIRECTIONS: Questions 6 through 8 are to be answered SOLELY on the basis of the following passage.

City governments have long had building codes which set minimum standards for building and for human occupancy. The code (or series of codes) makes provisions for standards of lighting and ventilation, sanitation, fire prevention, and protection. As a result of demands from manufacturers, builders, real estate people, tenement owners, and building-trades unions, these codes often have established minimum standards well below those that the contemporary society would accept as a rock-bottom minimum. Codes often become outdated so that meager standards in one era become seriously inadequate a few decades later as society"s concept of a minimum standard of living changes. Out-of-date codes, when still in use, have sometimes prevented the introduction of new devices and modern building techniques. Thus, it is extremely important that building codes keep pace with changes in the accepted concept of a minimum standard of living.

6. According to the above passage, all of the following considerations in building planning would probably be covered in a building code EXCEPT

    A. closet space as a percentage of total floor area
    B. size and number of windows required for rooms of differing sizes
    C. placement of fire escapes in each line of apartments
    D. type of garbage disposal units to be installed

7. According to the above passage, if an ideal building code were to be created, how would the established minimum standards in it compare to the ones that are presently set by city governments?
They would

    A. be lower than they are at present
    B. be higher than they are at present
    C. be comparable to the present minimum standards
    D. vary according to the economic group that sets them

8. On the basis of the above passage, what is the reason for difficulties in introducing new building techniques?

    A. Builders prefer techniques which represent the rock-bottom minimum desired by society.
    B. Certain manufacturers have obtained patents on various building methods to the exclusion of new techniques.
    C. The government does not want to invest money in techniques that will soon be outdated.
    D. New techniques are not provided for in building codes which are not up-to-date.

Questions 9-11.

DIRECTIONS: Questions 9 through 11 are to be answered SOLELY on the basis of the following paragraph.

When constructed within a multiple dwelling, such storage space shall be equipped with a sprinkler system and also with a system of mechanical ventilation in no way connected with any other ventilating system. Such storage space shall have no opening into any other part of the dwelling except through a fireproof vestibule. Any such vestibule shall have a minimum superficial floor area of fifty square feet, and its maximum area shall not exceed seventy-five square feet. It shall be enclosed with incombustible partitions having a fire-resistive rating of three hours. The floor and ceiling of such vestibule shall also be of incombustible material having a fire-resistive rating of at least three hours. There shall be two doors to provide access from the dwelling, to the car storage space. Each such door shall have a fire-resistive rating of one and one-half hours and shall be provided with a device to prevent the opening of one door until the other door is entirely closed.

9. According to the above paragraph, the one of the following that is REQUIRED in order for cars to be permitted to be stored in a multiple dwelling is a(n)

    A. fireproof vestibule   B. elevator from the garage
    C. approved heating system   D. sprinkler system

10. According to the above paragraph, the one of the following materials that would NOT be acceptable for the walls of a vestibule connecting a garage to the dwelling portion of a building is

   A. 3" solid gypsum blocks
   B. 4" brick
   C. 4" hollow gypsum blocks, plastered both sides
   D. 6" solid cinder concrete blocks

10.____

11. According to the above paragraph, the one of the following that would be ACCEPTABLE for the width and length of a vestibule connecting a garage that is within a multiple dwelling to the dwelling portion of the building is

   A. 3'8" x 13'0"
   B. 4'6" x 18'6"
   C. 4'9" x 14'6"
   D. 4'3" x 19'3"

11.____

Questions 12-13.

DIRECTIONS: Questions 12 and 13 are to be answered SOLELY on the basis of the following paragraph.

It shall be unlawful to place, use, or maintain in a condition intended, arranged, or designed for use, any gas-fired cooking appliance, laundry stove, heating stove, range or water heater or combination of such appliances in any room or space used for living or sleeping in any new or existing multiple dwelling unless such room or space has a window opening to the outer air or such gas appliance is vented to the outer air. All automatically operated gas appliances shall be equipped with a device which shall shut off automatically the gas supply to the main burners when the pilot light in such appliance is extinguished. A gas range or the cooking portion of a gas appliance incorporating a room heater shall not be deemed an automatically operated gas appliance. However, burners in gas ovens and broilers which can be turned on and off or ignited by non-manual means shall be equipped with a device which shall shut off automatically the gas supply to those burners when the operation of such non-manual means fails.

12. According to the above paragraph, an automatic shut-off device is NOT required on a gas

   A. hot water heater
   B. laundry dryer
   C. space heater
   D. range

12.____

13. According to the above paragraph, a gas-fired water heater is permitted

   A. only in kitchens
   B. only in bathrooms
   C. only in living rooms
   D. in any type of room

13.____

Questions 14-18.

DIRECTIONS: Questions 14 through 18 are to be answered SOLELY on the basis of the information contained in the statement below.

No multiple dwelling shall be erected to a height in excess of one and one-half times the width of the widest street on which it faces, except that above the level of such height, for each one foot that the front wall of such dwelling sets back from the street line, three feet shall be added to the height limit of such dwelling, but such dwelling shall not exceed in maximum height three feet plus one and three-quarter times the width of the widest street on which it faces.

Any such dwelling facing a street more than one hundred feet in width shall be subject to the same height limitations as though such dwelling faced a street one hundred feet in width.

14. The MAXIMUM height of a multiple dwelling set back five feet from the street line and facing a 60 foot wide street is _____ feet.   14.____

    A. 60   B. 90   C. 105   D. 165

15. The MAXIMUM height of a multiple dwelling set back six feet from the street line and facing a 120 foot wide street is _____ feet.   15.____

    A. 198   B. 168   C. 120   D. 105

16. The MAXIMUM height of a multiple dwelling is   16.____

    A. 100 ft.   B. 150 ft.   C. 178 ft.   D. unlimited

17. The MAXIMUM height of a multiple dwelling set back 10 feet from the street line and facing a 110 foot wide street is _____ feet.   17.____

    A. 178   B. 180   C. 195   D. 205

18. The MAXIMUM height of a multiple dwelling set back eight feet from the street line and facing a 90 foot wide street is _____ feet.   18.____

    A. 135   B. 147   C. 178   D. 159

Questions 19-23.

DIRECTIONS: Questions 19 through 23 are to be answered SOLELY on the basis of the following statement.

The number of persons accommodated on any story in a lodging house shall not be greater than the sum of the following components,

   a. 22 persons for each full multiple of 22 inches in the smallest clear width for each means of egress approved by the department, other than fire escapes
   b. 20 persons for each lawful fire escape accessible from such story.

19. The MAXIMUM number of persons that may be accommodated on a story in a lodging house depends on the   19.____

    A. number of lawful fire escapes *only*
    B. number of approved means of egress *only*
    C. smallest clear width in each approved means of egress *only*
    D. number of lawful fire escapes and sum total of smallest clear widths in each approved means of egress

20. The MAXIMUM number of persons that may be accommodated on a story of a lodging house having one lawful fire escape and a sum total of 44 inches in the smallest clear widths of the two approved means of egress is   20.____

    A. 20   B. 22   C. 42   D. 64

21. The MAXIMUM number of persons that may be accommodated on a story of a lodging house having two lawful fire escapes and a sum total of 60 inches in the smallest clear width of the approved means of egress is

    A. 64	B. 84	C. 100	D. 106

22. The MAXIMUM number of persons that may be accommodated on a story of a lodging house having one lawful fire escape and a sum total of 33 inches in the smallest clear width of the approved means of egress is

    A. 42	B. 53	C. 64	D. 73

23. The MAXIMUM number of persons that may be accommodated on a story of a lodging house having two lawful fire escapes and two approved means of egress, with 40 inches and 44 inches in the smallest clear widths, respectively, is

    A. 84	B. 104	C. 106	D. 108

Questions 24-25.

DIRECTIONS: Questions 24 and 25 are to be answered SOLELY on the basis of the following paragraph.

Though the recent trend toward apartment construction may appear to be the Region's response to large-lot zoning and centralized industry, it really is not. It is mainly a function of the age of the population. Most of the apartments are occupied by one- and two-person families young people out of school but without a family of their own and older people whose children have grown. Both groups have been increasing in number; and, in this Region, they characteristically live in apartments. It is this increased demand for apartments and the simultaneous decrease in demand for one-family houses that dramatically raised the percentage of building permits issued for multi-family housing units from 36 percent in 1977 to 67 percent in 1981. The fact that three-fourths of the apartments were built in the Core between 1977 and 1981 at the same time as the Core was losing population underscores the failure of the apartment boom to slow the outward spread of the population.

24. According to the above paragraph, one of the reasons for the increase in the number of building permits issued for multi-family construction in the City Metropolitan Region is

    A. that workers in industry want to live close to their jobs
    B. an increase in the number of elderly people living in the Region
    C. the inability of many families to afford the large lots necessary to build private homes
    D. the new zoning ordinance made it easier to build apartments

25. According to the above paragraph, the apartment construction boom

    A. increased the population density in the Core
    B. spurred a population shift to the suburbs
    C. did not halt the outward flow of the population from the Core
    D. was most significant in the outer areas of the Region

KEY (CORRECT ANSWERS)

1.	A	11.	C
2.	C	12.	D
3.	D	13.	D
4.	C	14.	C
5.	C	15.	B
6.	A	16.	C
7.	B	17.	A
8.	D	18.	D
9.	D	19.	D
10.	B	20.	D

21. B
22. A
23. C
24. B
25. C

TEST 2

DIRECTIONS: Each question or incomplete statement is followed by several suggested answers or completions. Select the one that BEST answers the question or completes the statement. *PRINT THE LETTER OF THE CORRECT ANSWER IN THE SPACE AT THE RIGHT.*

Questions 1-4.

DIRECTIONS: Questions 1 through 4 are to be answered SOLELY on the basis of the following paragraph.

Although the suburbs have provided housing and employment for millions of additional families since 1950, many suburban communities have maintained controls over the kinds of families who can live in them. Suburban attitudes have been formed by reaction against a perception of crowded, harassed city life and threatening alien city people. As population, taxable income, and jobs have left the cities for the suburbs, the *urban crisis* of substandard housing, declining levels of education and public services, and decreasing employment opportunities has been created. The crisis, however, is not urban at all, but national, and in part a result of the suburban policy that discourages outward movement by the urban poor.

1. According to the above paragraph, the quality of urban life

    A. is determined by public opinion in the cities
    B. has worsened in recent years
    C. is similar to rural life
    D. can be changed by political means

2. According to the above paragraph, suburban communities have

    A. tried to show that the urban crisis is really a national crisis
    B. avoided taking a position on the urban crisis
    C. been involved in causing the urban crisis
    D. been the innocent victims of the urban crisis

3. According to the above paragraph, the poor have

    A. become increasingly sophisticated in their attempts to move to the suburbs
    B. generally been excluded from the suburbs
    C. lost incentive for betterment of their living conditions
    D. sought improvement of the central cities

4. As used in the above paragraph, the word perception means MOST NEARLY

    A. development   B. impression
    C. opposition   D. uncertainty

Questions 5-8.

DIRECTIONS: Questions 5 through 8 are to be answered SOLELY on the basis of the following paragraph.

The concentration of publicly assisted housing in central cities -- because the suburbs do not want them and effectively bar them -- is usually rationalized by a solicitous regard for keeping intact the city neighborhoods cherished by low-income groups. If one accepted this as valid, the devotion of minorities to blighted city neighborhoods in preference to suburban employment and housing would be an historic first. Certainly no such devotion was visible among the millions who have deserted their city neighborhoods in the last 25 years even if it meant an arduous daily trip from the suburbs to their jobs in the cities.

5. The writer implies that MOST poor people

   A. prefer isolation
   B. fear change
   C. are angry
   D. seek betterment

6. The general tone of the paragraph is BEST characterized as

   A. uncertain   B. skeptical   C. evasive   D. indifferent

7. As used in the above paragraph, the word rationalize means MOST NEARLY

   A. dispute   B. justify   C. deny   D. locate

8. According to the above paragraph, publicly assisted housing is concentrated in the central cities PRIMARILY because

   A. city dwellers are unable to find satisfactory housing
   B. deterioration of older housing has increased in recent years
   C. suburbanites have opposed the movement of the poor to the suburbs
   D. employment opportunities have decreased in the suburbs

Questions 9-11.

DIRECTIONS: Questions 9 through 11 are to be answered SOLELY on the basis of the following paragraph.

In recent years, new and important emphasis has been placed upon the maximum use of conservation and rehabilitation techniques in carrying out programs of urban renewal and revitalization. In urban renewal projects where existing structures are hopelessly deteriorated or land uses are incompatible with the community's overall plans, the entire area may be acquired, cleared, and sold for redevelopment. However, where existing structures are basically sound but have deteriorated to the point where they are a blighting influence on the neighborhood, they may be salvaged through a program of rehabilitation and reconditioning.

9. According to the above paragraph, the one of the following which is MOST likely to cause area-wide razing of the buildings in urban renewal programs is

   A. a program of rehabilitation and reconditioning
   B. concerted insistence by landlords and tenants that certain buildings be bulldozed
   C. an inability of community groups to agree on priorities for staged clearance
   D. land use contrary to the community's general plan

10. According to the above paragraph, rehabilitation of structures may take place if

    A. new conservation and rehabilitation techniques are used
    B. salvaging all the buildings in the entire area is hopeless
    C. the community wishes to preserve historic structures
    D. the existing buildings are structurally sound

11. As used in the above paragraph, the word blighting means MOST NEARLY   11.____

    A. ruining   B. infrequent   C. recurrent   D. traditional

Questions 12-13.

DIRECTIONS: Questions 12 and 13 are to be answered SOLELY on the basis of the following paragraphs.

    We must also find better ways to handle the relocation of people uprooted by projects. In the past, many renewal plans have foundered on this problem, and it is still the most difficult part of the community development. Large-scale replacement of low-income residents -- many ineligible for public housing -- has contributed to deterioration of surrounding communities. However, thanks to changes in housing authority procedures, relocation has been accomplished in a far more satisfactory fashion. The step-by-step community development projects we advocate in this plan should bring further improvement.

    But additional measures will be necessary. There are going to be more people to be moved; and, with the current shortage of apartments, large ones especially, it is going to be tougher to find places to move them to. The city should have more freedom to buy or lease housing that comes on the market because of normal turnover and make it available to relocatees.

12. According to the above paragraphs, one of the reasons a neighborhood may deteriorate is that   12.____

    A. there is a scarcity of large apartments
    B. step-by-step community development projects have failed
    C. people in the given neighborhood are uprooted from their homes
    D. a nearby renewal project has an inadequate relocation plan

13. From the above paragraphs, one might conclude that the relocation phase of community renewal has been improved.   13.____

    A. by changes in housing authority procedures
    B. by development of step-by-step community development projects
    C. through expanded city powers to buy housing for relocation
    D. by the addition of huge sums of money

Questions 14-15.

DIRECTIONS: Questions 14 and 15 are to be answered SOLELY on the basis of the following paragraphs.

    Provision of decent housing for the lower half of the population (by income) was thus taken on as a public responsibility. Public housing was to assist the poorest quarter of urban families while the 221(d)(3) Housing Program would assist the next quarter. But limited funds meant that the supply of subsidized housing could not stretch nearly far enough to help this half of the population. Who were to be left out in the rationing process which was accomplished by the sifting of applicants for housing on the part of public and private authorities?

Discrimination on the grounds of race or color is not allowed under Federal law. In all sections of the country, encouragingly, housing programs are found which follow this law to the letter. Yet, housing programs in some cities still suffer from the residue of racial segregation policies and attitudes that for years were condoned or even encouraged.

Some sifting in the 221(d)(3) Housing Program follows the practice of many public housing authorities, the imposition of requirements with respect to character. This is a delicate matter. To fill a project overwhelmingly with broken families, alcoholics, criminals, delinquents, and other problem tenants would hardly make it a wholesome environment. Yet the total exclusion of such families is hardly an acceptable alternative. To the extent this exclusion is practiced, the very people whose lives are described in order to persuade lawmakers and the public to instigate new programs find the door shut in their faces when such programs come into being. The proper balance is difficult to achieve, but society's neediest families surely should not be totally denied the opportunities for rejuvenation in subsidized housing.

14. From the above paragraphs, it can be assumed that the 221(d)(3) Housing Program   14.____

    A. served a population earning more than the median income
    B. served a less affluent population than is served by public housing
    C. excludes all problem families from its projects
    D. is a subsidized housing program

15. According to this text, the provision of housing for the poor   15.____

    A. has not been completely accomplished with public monies
    B. is never influenced by segregationist policies
    C. is limited to providing housing for only the neediest families
    D. is primarily the responsibility of the Federal government

16. Five hundred persons attended a public hearing at which a proposed public housing project was being considered. Less than half favored the project while the majority opposed the project.   16.____
    According to the above statement, it is REASONABLE to conclude that

    A. the proposal stimulated considerable community interest
    B. the public housing project was disapproved by the city because a majority opposed it
    C. those who opposed the project lacked sympathy for needy persons
    D. the supporters of the project were led by militants

17. A vacant lot close to a polluted creek is for sale. Two buyers compete. One owns an adjacent factory which provides 300 high paying unskilled jobs. He needs to expand or move from the city. If he expands, he will provide 300 additional jobs. The other is a community group in a changing residential area close by. They hope to stabilize the neighborhood by bringing in new housing. They would build an apartment building with 100 dwelling units on the lot.   17.____
    According to the above paragraph, it is REASONABLE to conclude that

    A. jobs are more important than housing
    B. there is conflict between the factory owners and the neighborhood group
    C. the neighborhood group will not succeed in stabilizing the area by constructing new housing
    D. the polluted creek should be cleaned up

18. The housing authority faces every problem of the private developer, and it must also assume responsibilities of which private building is free. The authority must account to the community; it must conform to federal regulations; it must provide durable buildings of good standard at low cost; it must overcome the prejudices against public operations, of contractors, bankers, and prospective tenants. These authorities are being watched by anti-housing enthusiasts for the first error of judgment or the first evidence of high costs, to be torn to bits before a Congressional committee.
On the basis of this statement, it would be MOST correct to state that

   A. private builders do not have the opposition of contractors, bankers, and prospective tenants
   B. Congressional committees impede the progress of public housing by petty investigations
   C. a housing authority must deal with all the difficulties encountered by the private builder
   D. housing authorities are no more immune from errors in judgment than private developers

18._____

19. Another factor that has considerably added to the city's housing crisis has been the great influx of low-income workers and their families seeking better employment opportunities during wartime and defense boom periods. The circumstances of these families have forced them to crowd into the worst kind of housing and have produced on a renewed scale the conditions from which slums flourish and grow.
On the basis of this statement, one would be justified in stating that

   A. the influx of low-income workers has aggravated the slum problem
   B. the city has better employment opportunities than other sections of the country
   C. the high wages paid by our defense industries have made many families ineligible for tenancy in public housing projects
   D. the families who settled in the city during wartime and the defense build-up brought with them language and social customs conducive to the growth of slums

19._____

20. Much of the city felt the effects of the general postwar increase of vandalism and street crime, and the greatly expanded public housing program was no exception. Projects built in congested slum areas with a high incidence of delinquency and crime were particularly subjected to the depredations of neighborhood gangs. The civil service watchmen who patrolled the projects, unarmed and neither trained nor expected to perform police duties, were unable to cope with the situation.
On the basis of this statement, the MOST accurate of the following statements is:

   A. Neighborhood gangs were particularly responsible for the high incidence of delinquency and crime in congested slum areas having public housing programs
   B. Civil service watchmen who patrolled housing projects failed to carry out their assigned police duties
   C. Housing projects were not spared the effects of the general postwar increase of vandalism and street crime
   D. Delinquency and crime affected housing projects in slum areas to a greater extent than other dwellings in the same area

20._____

21. Another peculiar characteristic of real estate is the absence of liquidity. Each parcel is a discrete unit as to size, location, rental, physical condition, and financing arrangements. Each property requires investigation, comparison of rents with other properties, and individualized haggling on price and terms.
On the basis of this statement, the LEAST accurate of the following statements is:

    A. Although the size, location, and rent of parcels vary, comparison with rents of other properties affords an indication of the value of a particular parcel
    B. Bargaining skill is the essential factor in determining the value of a parcel of real estate
    C. Each parcel of real estate has individual peculiarities distinguishing it from any other parcel
    D. Real estate is not easily converted to other types of assets

21._____

22. In part, at least, the charges of sameness, monotony, and institutionalism directed at public housing projects result from the degree in which they differ from the city's normal housing pattern. They seem alike because their very difference from the usual makes them stand apart.
In many respects, there is considerably more variety between public housing projects than there is between different streets of apartment houses or tenements throughout the city.
On the basis of this statement, it would be LEAST accurate to state that:

    A. There is considerably more variety between public housing projects than there is between different streets of tenements throughout the city
    B. Public housing projects differ from the city's normal housing pattern to the degree that sameness, monotony, and institutionalism are characteristic of public buildings
    C. Public housing projects seem alike because their deviation from the usual dwellings draws attention to them
    D. The variety in structure between public housing projects and other public buildings is related to the period in which they were built

22._____

23. The amount of debt that can be charged against the city for public housing is limited by law. Part of the city's restricted housing means goes for cash subsidies it may be required to contribute to state-aided projects. Under the provisions of the state law, the city must match the state's contributions in subsidies; and while the value of the partial tax exemption granted by the city is counted for this purpose, it is not always sufficient.
On the basis of this statement, it would be MOST accurate to state that:

    A. The amount of money the city may spend for public housing is limited by annual tax revenues
    B. The value of tax exemptions granted by the city to educational, religious, and charitable institutions may be added to its subsidy contributions to public housing projects
    C. The subsidy contributions for state-aided public housing projects are shared equally by the state and the city under the provisions of the state law
    D. The tax revenues of the city, unless supplemented by state aid, are insufficient to finance public housing projects

23._____

24. Maintenance costs can be minimized and the useful life of houses can be extended by building with the best and most permanent materials available. The best and most permanent materials in many cases are, however, much more expensive than materials which require more maintenance. The most economical procedure in home building has been to compromise between the capital costs of high quality and enduring materials and the maintenance costs of less desirable materials.
On the basis of this statement, one would be justified in stating that:

    A. Savings in maintenance costs make the use of less durable and less expensive building materials preferable to high quality materials that would prolong the useful life of houses constructed from them
    B. Financial advantage can be secured by the home builder if he judiciously combines costly but enduring building materials with less desirable materials which, however, require more maintenance
    C. A compromise between the capital costs of high quality materials and the maintenance costs of less desirable materials makes it easier for a home builder to estimate construction expenditures
    D. The most economical procedure in home building is to balance the capital costs of the most permanent materials against the costs of less expensive materials that are cheaper to maintain

25. Personnel selection has been a critical problem for local housing authorities. The pool of qualified workers trained in housing procedures is small, and the colleges and universities have failed to grasp the opportunity for enlarging it. While real estate experience makes a good background for management of a housing project, many real estate men are deplorably lacking in understanding of social and governmental problems. Social workers, on the other hand, are likely to be deficient in business judgment.
On the basis of this statement, it would be MOST accurate to state that:

    A. Colleges and universities have failed to train qualified workers for proficiency in housing procedures
    B. Social workers are deficient in business judgment as related to the management of a housing project
    C. Real estate experience makes a person a good manager of a housing project
    D. Local housing authorities have been critical of present methods of personnel selection

KEY (CORRECT ANSWERS)

1.	B	11.	A
2.	C	12.	D
3.	B	13.	A
4.	B	14.	D
5.	D	15.	A
6.	B	16.	A
7.	B	17.	B
8.	D	18.	C
9.	D	19.	A
10.	D	20.	C

21. B
22. B
23. C
24. B
25. A

SUPERVISION STUDY GUIDE

Social science has developed information about groups and leadership in general and supervisor-employee relationships in particular. Since organizational effectiveness is closely linked to the ability of supervisors to direct the activities of employees, these findings are important to executives everywhere.

IS A SUPERVISOR A LEADER?

First-line supervisors are found in all large business and government organizations. They are the men at the base of an organizational hierarchy. Decisions made by the head of the organization reach them through a network of intermediate positions. They are frequently referred to as part of the management team, but their duties seldom seem to support this description.

A supervisor of clerks, tax collectors, meat inspectors, or securities analysts is not charged with budget preparation. He cannot hire or fire the employees in his own unit on his say-so. He does not administer programs which require great planning, coordinating, or decision making.

Then what is he? He is the man who is directly in charge of a group of employees doing productive work for a business or government agency. If the work requires the use of machines, the men he supervises operate them. If the work requires the writing of reports, the men he supervises write them. He is expected to maintain a productive flow of work without creating problems which higher levels of management must solve. But is he a leader?

To carry out a specific part of an agency's mission, management creates a unit, staffs it with a group of employees and designates a supervisor to take charge of them. Management directs what this unit shall do, from time to time changes directions, and often indicates what the group should not do. Management presumably creates status for the supervisor by giving him more pay, a title, and special privileges.

Management asks a supervisor to get his workers to attain organizational goals, including the desired quantity and quality of production. Supposedly, he has authority to enable him to achieve this objective. Management at least assumes that by establishing the status of the supervisor's position, it has created sufficient authority to enable him to achieve these goals— not his goals, nor necessarily the group's, but management's goals.

In addition, supervision includes writing reports, keeping records of membership in a higher-level administrative group, industrial engineering, safety engineering, editorial duties, housekeeping duties, etc. The supervisor as a member of an organizational network, must be responsible to the changing demands of the management above him. At the same time, he must be responsive to the demands of the work group of which he is a member. He is placed in the difficult position of communicating and implementing new decisions, changed programs and revised production quotas for his work group, although he may have had little part in developing them.

It follows, then, that supervision has a special characteristic: achievement of goals, previously set by management, through the efforts of others. It is in this feature of the supervisor's job that we find the role of a leader in the sense of the following definition: *A leader is that person who most effectively influences group activities toward goal setting and goal achievements.*

This definition is broad. It covers both leaders in groups that come together voluntarily and in those brought together through a work assignment in a factory, store, or government agency. In the natural group, the authority necessary to attain goals is determined by the group membership and is granted by them. In the working group, it is apparent that the establishment of a supervisory position creates a predisposition on the part of employees to accept the authority of the occupant of that position. We cannot, however, assume that mere occupation confers authority sufficient to assure the accomplishment of an organization's goals.

Supervision is different, then, from leadership. The supervisor is expected to fulfill the role of leader but without obtaining a grant of authority from the group he supervises. The supervisor is expected to influence the group in the achieving of goals but is often handicapped by having little influence on the organizational process by which goals are set. The supervisor, because he works in an organizational setting, has the burdens of additional organizational duties and restrictions and requirements arising out of the fact that his position is subordinate to a hierarchy of higher-level supervisors. These differences between leadership and supervision are reflected in our definition: *Supervision is basically a leadership role, in a formal organization, which has as its objective the effective influencing of other employees.*

Even though these differences between supervision and leadership exist, a significant finding of experimenters in this field is that supervisors must be leaders to be successful.

The problem is: How can a supervisor exercise leadership in an organizational setting? We might say that the supervisor is expected to be a natural leader in a situation which does not come about naturally. His situation becomes really difficult in an organization which is more eager to make its supervisors into followers rather than leaders.

LEADERSHIP: NATURAL AND ORGANIZATIONAL

Leadership, in its usual sense of *natural* leadership, and supervision are not the same. In some cases, leadership embraces broader powers and functions than supervision; in other cases, supervision embraces more than leadership. This is true both because of the organization and technical aspects of the supervisor's job and because of the relatively freer setting and inherent authority of the natural leader.

The natural leader usually has much more authority and influence than the supervisor. Group members not only follow his command but prefer it that way. The employee, however, can appeal the supervisor's commands to his union or to the supervisor's superior or to the personnel office. These intercessors represent restrictions on the supervisor's power to lead.

The natural leader can gain greater membership involvement in the group's objectives, and he can change the objectives of the group. The supervisor can attempt to gain employee support only for management's objectives; he cannot set other objectives. In these instances leadership is broader than supervision.

The natural leader must depend upon whatever skills are available when seeking to attain objectives. The supervisor is trained in the administrative skills necessary to achieve management's goals. If he does not possess the requisite skills, however, he can call upon management's technicians.

A natural leader can maintain his leadership, in certain groups, merely by satisfying members' need for group affiliation. The supervisor must maintain his leadership by directing and organizing his group to achieve specific organizational goals set for him and his group by management. He must have a technical competence and a kind of coordinating ability which is not needed by many natural leaders.

A natural leader is responsible only to his group which grants him authority. The supervisor is responsible to management, which employs him, and also to the work group of which he is a member. The supervisor has the exceedingly difficult job of reconciling the demands of two groups frequently in conflict. He is often placed in the untenable position of trying to play two antagonistic roles. In the above instance, supervision is broader than leadership.

ORGANIZATIONAL INFLUENCES ON LEADERSHIP

The supervisor is both a product and a prisoner of the organization wherein we find him. The organization which creates the supervisor's position also obstructs, restricts, and channelizes the exercise of his duties. These influences extend beyond prescribed functional relationships to specific supervisory behavior. For example, even in a face-to-face situation involving one of his subordinates, the supervisor's actions are controlled to a great extent by his organization. His behavior must conform to the organization policy on human relations, rules which dictate personnel procedures, specific prohibitions governing conduct, the attitudes of his own superior, etc. He is not a free agent operating within the limits of his work group. His freedom of action is much more circumscribed than is generally admitted. The organizational influences which limit his leadership actions can be classified as structure, prescriptions, and proscriptions.

The organizational structure places each supervisor's position in context with other designated positions. It determines the relationships between his position and specific positions which impinge on his. The structure of the organization designates a certain position to which he looks for orders and information about his work. It gives a particular status to his position within a pattern of statuses from which he perceives that (1) certain positions are on a par, organizationally, with his, (2) other positions are subordinate, and (3) still others are superior.

The organizational structure determines those positions to which he should look for advice and assistance, and those positions to which he should give advice and assistance.

For instance, the organizational structure has predetermined that the supervisor of a clerical processing unit shall report to a supervisory position in a higher echelon. He shall have certain relationships with the supervisors of the work units which transmit work to and receive work from his unit. He shall discuss changes and clarification of procedures with certain staff units, such as organization and methods, cost accounting, and personnel. He shall consult supervisors of units which provide or receive special work assignments.

The organizational structure, however, establishes patterns other than those of the relationships of positions. These are the patterns of responsibility, authority, and expectations.

The supervisor is responsible for certain activities or results; he is presumably invested with the authority to achieve these. His set of authority and responsibility is interwoven with other sets to the end that all goals and functions of the organization are parceled out in small, manageable lots. This, of course, establishes a series of expectations: a single supervisor can perform his particular set of duties only upon the assumption that preceding or contiguous sets of duties have been, or are being carried out. At the same time, he is aware of the expectations of others that he will fulfill his functional role.

The structure of an organization establishes relationships between specified positions and specific expectations for these positions. The fact that these relationships and expectations are established is one thing; whether or not they are met is another.

PRESCRIPTIONS AND PROSCRIPTIONS

But let us return to the organizational influences which act to restrict the supervisor's exercise of leadership. These are the prescriptions and proscriptions generally in effect in all organizations, and those peculiar to a single organization. In brief these are the *thou shalt's* and the *thou shalt not's*.

Organizations not only prescribe certain duties for individual supervisory positions, they also prescribe specific methods and means of carrying out these duties and maintaining management-employee relations. These include rules, regulations, policy, and tradition. It does no good for the supervisor to say, *This seems to be the best way to handle such-and-such,* if the organization has established a routine for dealing with problems. For good or bad, there are rules that state that firings shall be executed in such a manner, accompanied by a certain notification; that training shall be conducted, and in this manner. Proscriptions are merely negative prescriptions; you may not discriminate against any employee because of politics or race; you shall not suspend any employee without following certain procedures and obtaining certain approvals.

Most of these prohibitions and rules apply to the area of interpersonal relations, precisely the area which is now arousing most interest on the part of administrators and managers. We have become concerned about the contrast between formally prescribed relationships and interpersonal relationships, and this brings us to the often discussed informal organization.

FORMAL AND INFORMAL ORGANIZATIONS

As we well know, the functions and activities of any organization are broken down into individual units of work called positions. Administrators must establish a pattern which will link these positions to each other and relate them to a system of authority and responsibility. Man-to-man are spelled out as plainly as possible for all to understand. Managers, then, build an official structure which we call the formal organization.

In these same organizations, employees react individually and in groups to institutionally determined roles. John, a worker, rides in the same carpool as Joe, a foreman. An unplanned communication develops. Harry, a machinist knows more about high-speed machining than his foreman or anyone else in his shop. An unofficial tool boss comes into being. Mary, who fought with Jane, is promoted over her. Jane now gives Mary's directions. A planned relationship fails to develop. The employees have built a structure which we call the informal organization.

Formal organization is a system of management-prescribed relations between positions in an organization.

Informal organization is a network of unofficial relations between people in an organization.

These definitions might lead us to the absurd conclusion that positions carry out formal activities and that employe4es spend their time in unofficial activities. We must recognize that organizational activities are in all cases carried out by people. The formal structure provides a needed framework within which interpersonal relations occur. What we call informal organization is the complex of normal, natural relations among employees. These personal relationships may be negative or positive. That is, they may impede or aid the achievement of organizational goals. For example, friendship between two supervisors greatly increases the probability of good cooperation and coordination between their sections. On the other hand, *buck passing* nullifies the formal structure by failure to meet a prescribed and expected responsibility.

It is improbable that an ideal organization exists where all activities are carried out in strict conformity to a formally prescribed pattern of functional roles. Informal organization arises because of the incompleteness and ambiguities in the network of formally prescribed relationships, or in response to the needs or inadequacies of supervisors or managers who hold prescribed functional roles in an organization. Many of these relationships are not prescribed by the organizational pattern; many cannot be prescribed; many should not be prescribed.

Management faces the problem of keeping the informal organization in harmony with the mission of the agency. One way to do this is to make sure that all employees have a clear understanding of and are sympathetic with that mission. The issuance of organizational charts, procedural manuals, and functional descriptions of the work to be done by divisions and sections helps communicate management's plans and goals. Issuances alone, of course, cannot do the whole job. They should be accompanied by oral discussion and explanation. Management must ensure that there is mutual understanding and acceptance of charts and procedures. More important is that management acquaint itself with the attitudes, activities, and peculiar brands of logic which govern the informal organization. Only through this type of knowledge can they and supervisors keep informal goals consistent with the agency mission.

SUPERVISION STATUS AND FUNCTIONAL ROLE

A well-established supervisor is respected by the employees who work with him. They defer to his wishes. It is clear that a superior-subordinate relationship has been established. That is, status of the supervisor has been established in relation to other employees of the same work group. This same supervisor gains the respect of employees when he behaves in as certain manner. He will be expected, generally, to follow the customs of the group in such matters as dress, recreation, and manner of speaking. The group has a set of expectations as to his behavior. His position is a functional role which carries with it a collection of rights and obligations.

The position of supervisor usually has a status distinct from the individual who occupies it: it is much like a position description which exists whether or not there is an incumbent. The status of a supervisory position is valued higher than that of an employee position both because of the functional role of leadership which is assigned to it and because of the status symbols of titles, rights, and privileges which go with it.

Social ranking, or status, is not simple because it involves both the position and the man. An individual may be ranked higher than others because of his education, social background, perceived leadership ability, or conformity to group customs and ideals. If such a man is ranked higher by the members of a work group than their supervisor, the supervisor's effectiveness may be seriously undermined.

If the organization does not build and reinforce a supervisor's status, his position can be undermined in a different way. This will happen when managers go around rather than through the supervisor or designate him as a straw boss, acting boss, or otherwise not a real boss.

Let us clarify this last point. A role, and corresponding status, establishes a set of expectations. Employees expect their supervisor to do certain things and to act in certain ways. They are prepared to respond to that expected behavior. When the supervisor's behavior does not conform to their expectations, they are surprised, confused, and ill-at-ease. It becomes necessary for them to resolve their confusion, if they can. They might do this by turning to one of their own members for leadership. If the confusion continues, or their attempted solutions are not satisfactory, they will probably become a poorly motivated, non-cohesive group which cannot function very well.

COMMUNICATION AND THE SUPERVISOR

In a recent survey, railroad workers reported that they rarely look to their supervisor for information about the company. This is startling, at least to us, because we ordinarily think of the supervisor as the link between management and worker. We expect the supervisor to be the prime source of information about the company. Actually, the railroad workers listed the supervisor next to last in the o5rder of their sources of information. Most surprising of all, the supervisors, themselves, stated that rumor and unofficial contacts were their principal sources of information. Here we see one of the reasons why supervisors may not be as effective as management desires.

The supervisor is not only being bypassed by his work group, he is being ignored, and his position weakened, by the very organization which is holding him responsible for the activities of his workers. If he is management's representative to the employee, then management has an obligation to keep him informed of its activities. This is necessary if he is to carry out his functions efficiently and maintain his leadership in the work group. The supervisor is expected to be a source of information; when he is not, his status is not clear, and employees are dissatisfied because he has not lived up to expectations.

By providing information to the supervisor to pass along to employees, we can strengthen his position as leader of the group, and increase satisfaction and cohesion within the group. Because he has more information than the other members, receives information sooner, and passes it along at the proper times, members turn to him as a source and also provide him with information in the hope of receiving some in return. From this, we can see an increase in group cohesiveness because:

- Employees are bound closer to their supervisor because he is *in the know.*
- There is less need to go outside the group for answers
- Employees will more quickly turn to the supervisor for enlightenment

The fact that he has the answers will also enhance the supervisor's standing in the eyes of his men. This increased status will serve to bolster his authority and control of the group and will probably result in improved morale and productivity.

The foregoing, of course, does not mean that all management information should be given out. There are obviously certain policy determinations and discussions which need not or cannot be transmitted to all supervisors. However, the supervisor must be kept as fully informed as possible so that he can answer questions when asked and can allay needless fears and anxieties. Further, the supervisor has the responsibility of encouraging employee questions and submissions of information. He must be able to present information to employees so that it is clearly understood and accepted. His attitude and manner should make it clear that he believes in what he is saying, that the information is necessary or desirable to the group, and that he is prepared to act on the basis of the information.

SUPERVISION AND JOB PERFORMANCE

The productivity of work groups is a product; employees' efforts are multiplied by the supervision they receive. Many investigators have analyzed this relationship and have discovered elements of supervision which differentiate high and low production groups. These researchers have identified certain types of supervisory practices which they classify as *employee-centered* and other types which they classify as *production centered*.

The difference between these two kinds of supervision lies not in specific practices but in the approach or orientation to supervision. The employee-centered supervisor directs most of his efforts toward increasing employee motivation. He is concerned more with realizing the potential energy of persons than with administrative and technological methods of increasing efficiency and productivity. He is the man who finds ways of causing employees to want to work harder with the same tools. These supervisors emphasize the personal relations between their employees and themselves.

Now, obviously, these pictures are overdrawn. No one supervisor has all the virtues of the ideal type of employee-centered supervisor. And, fortunately, no one supervisor has all the bad traits found in many production-centered supervisors. We should remember that the various practices that researchers have fond which distinguish these two kinds of supervision represent the many practices and methods of supervisors of all gradations between these extremes. We should be careful, too, of the implications of the labels attached to the two types. For instance, being production-centered is not necessarily bad, since the principal responsibility of any supervisor is maintaining the production level that is expected of his work group. Being employee-centered may not necessarily be good, if the only result is a happy, chuckling crew of loafers. To return to the researchers' findings, employee-centered supervisors:

- Recommend promotions, transfers, pay increases
- Inform men about what is happening in the company
- Keep men posted on how well they are doing
- Hear complaints and grievances sympathetically
- Speak up for subordinates

Production-centered supervisors, on the other hand, don't do those things. They check on employees more frequently, give more detailed and frequent instructions, don't give reasons for changes, and are more punitive when mistakes are made. Employee-centered supervisors were reported to contribute to high morale and high production, whereas production-centered supervision was associated with lower morale and less production.

More recent findings, however, show that the relationship between supervision and productivity is not this simple. Investigators now report that high production is more frequently associated with supervisory practices which combine employee-centered behavior with concern for production. (This concern is not the same, however, as anxiety about production, which is the hallmark of our production-centered supervisor.) Let us examine these apparently contradictory findings and the premises from which they are derived.

SUPERVISION AND MORALE

Why do supervisory activities cause high or low production? As the name implies, the activities of the employee-centered supervisor tend to relate him more closely and satisfactorily to his workers. The production-centered supervisor's practices tend to separate him from his group and to foster antagonism. An analysis of this difference may answer our question.

Earlier, we pointed out that the supervisor is a type of leader and that leadership is intimately related to the group in which it occurs We discover, now, that an employee-centered supervisor's primary activities are concerned with both his leadership and his group membership. Such a supervisor is a member of a group and occupies a leadership role in that group.

These facts are sometimes obscured when we speak of the supervisor as management's representative, or as the organizational link between management and the employee, or as the end of the chain of command. If we really want to understand what it is we expect of the supervisor, we must remember that he is the designated leader of a group of employees to whom he is bound by interaction and interdependence.

Most of his actions are aimed, consciously or unconsciously, at strengthening membership ties in the group. This includes both making members more conscious that he is a member of their group) and causing members to identify themselves more closely with the group. These ends are accomplished by:

- making the group more attractive to the worker: they find satisfaction of their needs for recognition, friendship, enjoyable work, etc.;
- maintaining open communication: employees can express their views and obtain information about the organization
- giving assistance: members can seek advice on personal problems as well as their work; and
- acting as a buffer between the group and management: he speaks up for his men and explains the reasons for management's decisions.

Such actions both strengthen group cohesiveness and solidarity and affirm the supervisor's leadership position in the group.

DEFINING MORALE

This brings us back to a point mentioned earlier. We had said that employee-centered supervisors contribute to high morale as well as to high production. But how can we explain units which have low morale and high productivity, or vice versa? Usually production and morale are considered separately, partly because they are measured against different criteria and partly because, in some instances, they seem to be independent of each other.

Some of this difficulty may stem from confusion over definitions of morale. Morale has been defined as, or measured by, absences from work, satisfaction with job or company, dissension among members of work groups, productivity, apathy or lack of interest, readiness to help others, and a general aura of happiness as rated by observers. Some of these criteria of morale are not subject to the influence of the supervisor, and some of them are not clearly related to productivity. Definitions like these invite findings of low morale coupled with high production.

Both productivity and morale can be influenced by environmental factors not under the control of group members or supervisors. Such things as plant layout, organizational structure and goals, lighting, ventilation, communications, and management planning may have an adverse or desirable effect.

We might resolve the dilemma by defining morale on the basis of our understanding of the supervisor as leader of a group; morale is the degree of satisfaction of group members with their leadership. In this light, the supervisor's employee-centered activities bear a clear relation to morale. His efforts to increase employee identification with the group and to strengthen his leadership lead to greater satisfaction with that leadership. By increasing group cohesiveness and by demonstrating that his influence and power can aid the group, he is able to enhance his leadership status and afford satisfaction to the group.

SUPERVISION, PRODUCTION, AND MORALE

There are factors within the organization itself which determine whether increased production is possible:

- Are production goals expressed in terms understandable to employees and are they realistic?
- Do supervisors responsible for production respect the agency mission and production goals?
- If employees do not know how to do the job well, does management provide a trainer—often the supervisor—who can teach efficient work methods?

There are other factors within the work group which determine whether increased production will be attained:

- Is leadership present which can bring about the desired level of production?
- Are production goals accepted by employees as reasonable and attainable?
- If group effort is involved, are members able to coordinate their efforts?

Research findings confirm the view that an employee-centered supervisor can achieve higher morale than a production-centered supervisor. Managers may well ask what is the relationship between this and production.

Supervision is production-oriented to the extent that it focuses attention on achieving organizational goals, and plans and devises methods for attaining them; it is employee-centered to the extent that it focuses attention on employee attitudes toward those goals, and plans and works toward maintenance of employee satisfaction.

High productivity and low morale result when a supervisor plans and organizes work efficiently but cannot achieve high membership satisfaction. Low production and high morale result when a supervisor, though keeping members satisfied with his leadership, either has not gained acceptance of organizational goals or does not have the technical competence to achieve them.

The relationship between supervision, morale, and productivity is an interdependent one, with the supervisor playing an integral role due to his ability to influence productivity and morale independently of each other.

A supervisor who can plan his work well has good technical knowledge, and who can install better production methods can raise production without necessarily increasing group satisfaction. On the other hand, a supervisor who can motivate his employees and keep them satisfied with his leadership can gain high production in spite of technical difficulties and environmental obstacles.

CLIMATE AND SUPERVISION

Climate, the intangible environment of an organization made up of attitudes, beliefs, and traditions, plays a large part in morale, productivity, and supervision. Usually when we speak of climate and its relationship to morale and productivity, we talk about the merits of *democratic* versus *authoritarian* climate. Employees seem to produce more and have higher morale in a democratic climate, whereas in an authoritarian climate, the reverse seems to be true or so the researchers tell us. We would do well to determine what these terms mean to supervision.

Perhaps most of our difficulty in understanding and applying these concepts comes from our emotional reactions to the words themselves. For example, authoritarian climate is usually painted as the very blackest kind of dictatorship. This is not surprising, because we are usually expected to believe that it is invariably bad. Conversely, democratic climate is drawn to make the driven snow look impure by comparison.

Now these descriptions are most probably true when we talk about our political processes, or town meetings, or freedom of speech. However, the same labels have been used by social scientists in other contexts and have also been applied to government and business organizations, without it, it seems, any recognition that the meanings and their social values may have changed somewhat

For example, these labels were used in experiments conducted in an informal classroom setting using 11-year-old boys as subjects. The descriptive labels applied to the climate of the setting as well as the type of leadership practiced. When these labels were transferred to a management setting, it seems that many presumed that they principally meant the king of leadership rather than climate. We can see that there is a great difference between the experimental and management settings and that leadership practices for one might be inappropriate for the other.

It is doubtful that formal work organizations can be anything but authoritarian, in that goals are set by management and a hierarchy exists through which decisions and orders from the top are transmitted downward. Organizations are authoritarian by structure and need; direction and control are placed in the hands of a few in order to gain fast and efficient decision making. Now this does not mean to describe a dictatorship. It is merely the recognition of the fact that direction of organizational affairs comes from above. It should be noted that leadership in some natural groups is, in this sense, authoritarian.

Granting that formal organizations have this kind of authoritarian leadership, can there be a democratic climate? Certainly there can be, but we would want to define and delimit this term. A more realistic meaning of democratic climate in organizations is the use of permissive and participatory methods in management-employee relations. That is, a mutual exchange of information and explanation with the granting of individual freedom within certain restricted and defined limits. However, it is not our purpose to debate the merits of authoritarianism versus democracy. We recognize that within the small work group there is a need for freedom from constraint and an increase in participation in order to achieve organizational goals within the framework of the organizational movement.

Another aspect of climate is best expressed by this familiar, and true, saying: actions speak louder than words. Of particular concern to us is this effect of management climate on the behavior of supervisors, particularly in employee-centered activities.

There have been reports of disappointment with efforts to make supervisors ore employee-centered. Managers state that, since research has shown ways of improving human relations, supervisors should begin to practice these methods. Usually a training course in human relations is established; and supervisors are given this training. Managers then sit back and wait for the expected improvements, only to find that there are none.

If we wish to produce changes in the supervisor's behavior, the climate must be made appropriate and rewarding to the changed behavior. This means that top-level attitudes and behavior cannot deny or contradict the change we are attempting to effect. Basic changes in organizational behavior cannot be made with any permanence, unless we provide an environment that is receptive to the changes and rewards those persons who do change.

IMPROVING SUPERVISION

Anyone who has read this far might expect to find *A Dozen Rules for Dealing With Employees* or *29 Steps to Supervisory Success*. We will not provide such a list.

Simple rules suffer from their simplicity. They ignore the complexities of human behavior. Reliance upon rules may cause supervisors to concentrate on superficial aspects of their relations with employees. It may preclude genuine understanding.

The supervisor who relies on a list of rules tends to think of people in mechanistic terms. In a certain situation, he uses *Rule No. 3*. Employees are not treated as thinking and feeling persons, but rather as figures in a formula: Rule 3 applied to employee X = Production.

Employees usually recognize mechanical manipulation and become dissatisfied and resentful. They lose faith in, and respect for, their supervisor, and this may be reflected in lower morale and productivity.

We do not mean that supervisors must become social science experts if they wish to improve. Reports of current research indicate that there are two major parts of their job which can be strengthened through self-improvement: (1) Work planning, including technical skills, and (2) motivation of employees.

The most effective supervisors combine excellence in the administrative and technical aspects of their work with friendly and considerate personal relations with their employees.

CRITICAL PERSONAL RELATIONS

Later in this chapter we shall talk about administrative aspects of supervision, but first let us comment on *friendly and considerate personal relations*. We have discussed this subject throughout the preceding chapters, but we want to review some of the critical supervisory influences on personal relations.

Closeness of Supervision: The closeness of supervision has an important effect on productivity and morale. Mann and Dent found that supervisors of low-producing units supervise very closely, while high-producing supervisors exercise only general supervision. It was found that the low-producing supervisors:

- check on employees more frequently
- give more detailed and frequent instructions
- limit employee's freedom to do job in own way

Workers who felt less closely supervised reported that they were better satisfied with their jobs and the company. We should note that the manner or attitude of the supervisor has an important bearing on whether employees perceive supervision as being close or general.

These findings are another way of saying that supervision does not mean standing over the employee and telling him what to do and when and how to do it. The more effective supervisor tells his employees what is required, giving general instructions.

COMMUNICATION

Supervisors of high-production units consider communication as one of the most important aspects of their job. Effective communication is used by these supervisors to achieve better interpersonal relations and improved employee motivation. Low-production supervisors do not rate communications as highly important.

High-producing supervisors find that an important aid to more effective communication is listening. They are ready to listen to both personal problems or interests and questions about the work. This does not mean that they are *nosey* or meddle in their employees' personal lives, but rather that they show a willingness to listen, and do listen, if their employees wish to discuss problems.

These supervisors inform employees about forthcoming changes in work; they discuss agency policy with employees; and they make sure that each employee knows how well he is doing. What these supervisors do is use two-way communication effectively. Unless the supervisor freely imparts information, he will not receive information in return.

Attitudes and perception are frequently affected by communication or the lack of it. Research surveys reveal that many supervisors are not aware of their employees' attitudes, nor do they know what personal reactions their supervision arouses. Through frank discussion with employees, they have been surprised to discover employee beliefs about which they were ignorant. Discussion sometimes reveals that the supervisor and his employees have totally different impressions about the same event. The supervisor should be constantly on the alert for misconceptions about his words and deeds. He must remember that, although his actions are perfectly clear to himself, they may be, and frequently are, viewed differently by employees.

Failure to communicate information results in misconceptions and false assumptions. What you say and how you say it will strongly affect your employees' attitudes and perceptions. By giving them available information, you can prevent misconceptions; by discussion, you may be able to change attitudes; by questioning, you can discover what the perceptions and assumptions really are. And it need hardly be added that actions should conform very closely to words.

If we were to attempt to reduce the above discussion on communication to rules, we would have a long list which would be based on one cardinal principle: Don't make assumptions!

- Don't assume that your employees know; tell them.
- Don't assume that you know how they feel; find out.
- Don't assume that they understand; clarify.

20 SUPERVISORY HINTS

1. Avoid inconsistency.
2. Always give employees a chance to explain their action before taking disciplinary action. Don't allow too much time for a "cooling off" period before disciplining an employee.
3. Be specific in your criticisms.
4. Delegate responsibility wisely.
5. Do not argue or lose your temper, and avoid being impatient.
6. Promote mutual respect and be fair, impartial, and open-minded.
7. Keep in mind that asking for employees' advice and input can be helpful in decision making.
8. If you make promises, keep them.
9. Always keep the feelings, abilities, dignity and motives of your staff in mind.
10. Remain loyal to your employees' interests.
11. Never criticize employees in front of others, or treat employees like children.
12. Admit mistakes. Don't place blame on your employees, or make excuses.
13. Be reasonable in your expectations, give complete instructions, and establish well-planned goals.
14. Be knowledgeable about office details and procedures, but avoid becoming bogged down in details.
15. Avoid supervising too closely or too loosely. Employees should also view you as an approachable supervisor.
16. Remember that employees' personal problems may affect job performance, but become involved only when appropriate.
17. Work to develop workers, and to instill a feeling of cooperation while working toward mutual goals.
18. Do not overpraise or underpraise, be properly appreciative.
19. Never ask an employee to discipline someone for you.
20. A complaint, even if unjustified, should be taken seriously.

NOTES

ZONING ORDINANCES IN RELATION TO THE HOUSING INSPECTION

	Page
I. Background of Zoning	1
II. Definitions	2
III. Zoning Objectives	3
IV. What Zoning Cannot Do	4
V. Content of the Ordinance	4
VI. Bulk and Height requirements	5
VII. Yard Requirements	5
VIII. Off street Parking	6
IX. Nonconforming Uses	6
X. Variances	6
XI. Exceptions	7
XII. Administration	7
XIII. How Zoning Can Benefit the Housing Inspector	7
XIV. Example of Zoning and Housing Relationships	8

ZONING ORDINANCES IN RELATION TO THE HOUSING INSPECTION

Zoning is essentially a means of ensuring that a community's hind uses are compatibly located for the health, safety, and general welfare of the community. Experience has shown that some types of controls are needed in order to provide orderly growth in relation to the community plan for development. Just as a capital improvement program governs public improvements such as streets, parks, and other recreational facilities, schools, and public buildings, so zoning governs the planning program with respect to the use of public and private property.

When a person buys or builds a house or other structure in a municipality that has a zoning ordinance in effect, he is presumed to know and obliged by law to comply with the zoning regulations governing the use of buildings and land in the section of the community in which his property is located. If he either erects a structure or converts a house or building that is within that particular district by the local zoning ordinance into another type of use he still has acquired no property right to continue the forbidden use. An example would be the conversion of a single family residence into multifamily units. Even if the owner has obtained a building permit for this work already completed, the building permit would be voided, because the work was started in violation of the zoning code and because a building permit can be valid' only when issued for a lawful purpose. The building inspector is therefore obliged to refuse issuance of a building permit if the proposed work is in violation of the zoning ordinance.

It is very important that the housing inspector know the general nature of zoning regulations, since properties in violation of both the housing code and the zoning ordinance must be brought into full compliance with the zoning ordinance before the housing code can be enforced. In many cases the housing inspector may be able to eliminate some of the properties in violation of the housing code through enforcement of the zoning ordinance.

I. Background of Zoning

Zoning regulations have been used for several centuries. In the early settlement of our country, gunpowder mills and storehouses were prohibited from being located within the heavily populated portions of town, owing to the frequent fires and explosions. Later, zoning took the form of fire districts, and under implied legislative powers, wooden buildings were prohibited from certain sections of the municipality.

Massachusetts passed one of the first zoning laws in 1692. This law authorized Boston, Salem, Charlestown, and certain other market towns in the province to assign certain locations in each town for the establishment of slaughterhouses and still houses for currying of leather.

Act and Resolves of the Province of Massachusetts Bay 1692-93 C. 23

"Be it ordained and enacted by the Governor, Council and Representatives convened in General Court or Assembly, and by the authority of the same,

Sect. 1 That the selectmen of the towns of Boston, Salem, and Charlestown respectively, or other market towns in the province, with two or more justices of the peace dwelling in the town, or two of the next justices of the country, shall at or before the last day of March, one thousand six hundred ninety-three, assign some certain places of the said towns (where it may be least offensive) for the erecting or setting up of slaughterhouses for the killing of all meat, still houses, and houses for trying of tallow and currying of leather (which houses may be erected of timber, the law referring to building with brick or stone not withstanding) and shall cause an entry to be made in the town book of what places shall be by them so assigned, and make known the same by posting it up in some public places of the town; by which houses and places respectively, and no other, all butchers, slaughter men, distillers, chandlers, and curriers shall exercise and practice their respective trades and mysteries; on pain that any butcher or slaughter man transgressing of this act by killing of meat in any other place, for every conviction thereof before one or more justices of the peace, shall forfeit and pay the sum of twenty shillings (shilling worth about 12-16¢); and any distiller, chandler or currier offending against this act, for every conviction thereof before their majesties justices at the general sessions of the peace for the county, shall forfeit and pay the sum of five pounds (a pound equals 20 shillings and was worth somewhere between $2.40 and $3.20); one-third part of said forfeitures to be the use of the majesties for the support of the government of the province and incident charges thereof, one-third to the poor of the town when such offense shall be committed, and the other third to him or them that shall inform and sue for the same ....

II. Definitions

A. Accessory Structure - A detached building or structure in a secondary or subordinate capacity from the main or principal building or structure on the same premises. Example: garage behind a single-family dwelling.

B. Accessory Use - A use incidental and subordinate to the principal use of a structure. Example: a home-located physician's office.

C. Alteration - A change or rearrangement of the structural parts of a building, or an expansion or enlargement of the building.

D. Building Area - That portion of the lot remaining available for construction after all required open space and yard requirements are met.

E. Dwelling - Any enclosed space that is wholly or partially used or intended to be used for living or sleeping by human occupants provided that temporary housing shall not be regarded as a dwelling. Temporary housing is defined as any tent, trailer, mobile home, or any other shelter designed to be transportable and not attached to the ground, to another structure, or to any utility system on the same premises for more than 30 consecutive days.

F. Dwelling, Two Family - A structure containing two dwelling units and designed for occupancy by no more than two families.

G. Dwelling, Multifamily - A residential structure equipped with more than two dwelling units.

H. Dwelling Unit - Any room or group of rooms located within a dwelling and forming a single habitable unit with facilities that are used or intended to be used by a single family for living, sleeping, cooking, and eating.

I. Exception - Sometimes called "special use." An exception is a land use that can be made compatible with a district upon the imposition by the board of adjustment of special provisions covering its development, even though it would not otherwise be permitted in the district. Example: Fire substation being permitted to locate in a residential area.

J. Family - One or more individuals living together and sharing common living, sleeping, cooking, and eating facilities.

K. Home Occupation - An occupation conducted in a dwelling unit subject to the restrictions of the zoning ordinance. Limitations of interest to housing inspectors are the following: (a) Only the occupant or members of his family residing on the premises shall be engaged in the occupation, (b) the home occupation use shall be subordinate to its use for residential purposes and shall not occupy more than 25 per cent of the floor area of the dwelling unit, (c) the home occupation shall not be conducted in an accessory structure, (d) no offensive noise, glare, vibration, heat, smoke, dust, or odor shall be produced.

L. Lot- Parcel of land considered as a unit devoted to either a particular use or to occupancy by a building and its accessory structures.

M. Lot Depth - The average horizontal distance between the front and rear lot line measured at right angles to the structure.

N. Lot Width - The average horizontal distance between the sides of a lot measured at right angles to the lot depth.

O. Nonconforming Use - (a) Use of a building or use of land that does not conform to the regulations of the district in which located. (b) Nonconforming use also means a building or land use that does not conform to the regulations of the district in which the building or land is but that is nevertheless legal since it existed before enactment of the ordinance.

P. Open Space - Unoccupied space that is open to the sky and on the same lot with the building.

Q. Variance - Easing or lessening of the terms of the zoning ordinance by a public body so that relief for hardships will be provided but with the public interest still protected.

Inspectors should refer to the definitions in the zoning ordinance of their municipality for additions and changes.

III. Zoning Objectives

As stated earlier, the purpose of a zoning ordinance is to ensure that the land uses within the community are regulated not only for the health, safety, and welfare of the community but also in keeping with the comprehensive plan for community development. The objectives contained in the zoning ordinance that help to achieve a development providing for the health, safety, and welfare are the following:

A. Regulate Height, Bulk, and Area of Structure. In order to provide established standards of healthful housing within the community, regulations dealing with building heights, lot coverage, and floor areas must be established. These regulations then ensure that adequate natural lighting, ventilation, privacy, and recreational area for children will be realized. These are all fundamental physiological needs that have been determined to be necessary for a healthful environment.

Safety from fires is enhanced because of building separations needed to meet yard and open-space requirements.

Through prescribing minimum lot area per dwelling unit, population density controls are established.

B. Avoid Undue Levels of Noise, Vibration, Glare, Air Pollution, and Odor. By providing land use category districts, these environmental stresses upon the individual can be reduced. As in the first item, the absence of these stresses has been determined to be a fundamental physiological individual need.

C. Lessen Street Congestion Through Off-Street Parking and Off-Street Loading Requirement.

D. Facilitate Adequate Provisions of Water, Sewerage, Schools, Parks, and Playgrounds.

E. Secure Safety From Flooding.

F. Conserve Property Values. Through careful enforcement of the provisions property values will be stabilized and conserved.

IV. What Zoning Cannot Do

In order to understand more fully the difference between zoning and the other devices such as subdivision regulations, building codes, and housing ordinances, the housing inspector must know the things that cannot be accomplished by a zoning ordinance.

Items that cannot be accomplished in a zoning ordinance include:

A. Correcting Existence of Overcrowding or Substandard Housing. Zoning is not retroactive and cannot correct conditions such as those cited. These are corrected through enforcement of a minimum standards housing code.

B. Materials and Methods of Construction. Materials and methods of construction are enforced through the building codes rather than through zoning.

C. Cost of Construction. Quality of construction and hence construction costs are often regulated through deed restrictions or covenants. Zoning does, however, stabilize property values in an area by prohibiting incompatible development such as the location of a heavy industry in the midst of a well-established subdivision.

D. Subdivision Design and Layout. Design and layout of subdivisions as well as provisions for parks and streets are controlled through subdivision regulations.

V. Content of the Ordinance

Zoning ordinances establish districts of whatever size, shape, and number the municipality deems best for carrying out the purposes of the zoning ordinance. Most cities use three major districts: residential, commercial, and industrial. These three may then be subdivided into many sub districts, depending on local conditions. These districts specify the principal and accessory uses, exceptions, and prohibitions.

In general these permitted land uses are based on intensity of land use, a less intense land use being permitted in a more intense district but not vice versa. For example, a single-family residence is a less intense land use than a multifamily dwelling. A multifamily dwelling would not, however, be permitted in a single-family district.

In recent years, some ordinances are being partially based on performance standards rather than solely on land use intensity. For example, some types of industrial developments may be permitted in a less intense use district provided that the proposed land use creates no noise, glare, smoke, dust, vibration, or other environmental stress exceeding acceptable standards and provided further that adequate off street parking, screening, landscaping, and other similar measures are taken.

VI. Bulk and Height Requirements

To further achieve the earlier stated objectives of the zoning ordinance, other regulations within a particular zoning district are imposed to gain control of population densities and to provide adequate light, air, privacy, and other elements needed for a safe and healthy environment.

Most early zoning ordinances stated that within a particular district the height and bulk of any structure could not exceed certain dimensions and specified that dimensions for front, side, and rear yards must be provided. Today some zoning ordinances use floor area ratios for regulation. Floor area ratio is the relationship between the floor space of the structure and the size of the lot on which it is located. For example, a floor area ratio of 1 would permit either a two-story building covering 50 per cent of the lot, or a one-story building covering 100 per cent of the lot. This is illustrated in Figure 1. Other zoning ordinances specify the maximum amount of the lot that can be covered or else merely require that a certain amount of open space must be provided for each structure and leave the flexibility of the location to the builder. Still other ordinances, rather than specify a particular height for the structure, specify an angle of light obstruction within a particular district that will assure air and light to the surrounding structures. An example of this is shown in Figure 2.

VII. Yard Requirements

Zoning ordinances also contain yard requirements that are divided into front, rear, and side yard requirements. These requirements, in addition to stating the lot dimensions, usually designate the amount of setback

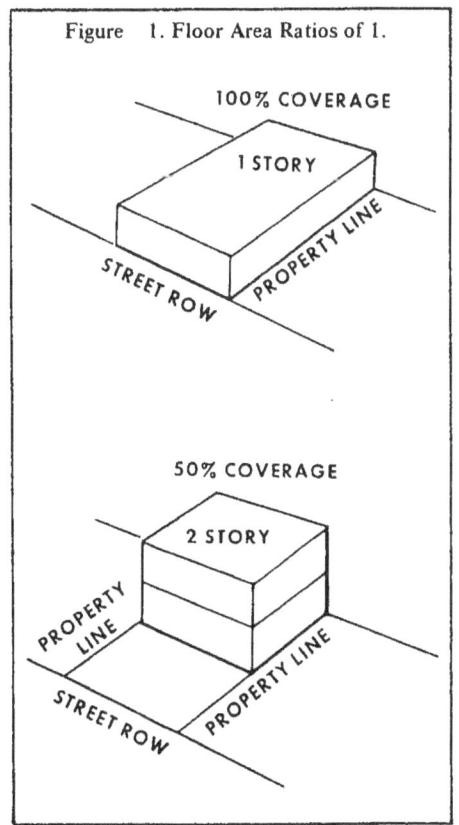

Figure 1. Floor Area Ratios of 1.

required. Most ordinances permit the erection of auxiliary buildings in rear yards provided they are located at stated distances from all lot lines and provided sufficient stated open space is maintained. If the property is a corner lot, additional requirements are set to allow visibility for motorists.

VIII. Off street Parking

Space for off street parking and off street loading is also contained in the ordinance. These requirements are based on standards relating floor space or seating capacity to land use. For example, a furniture store would require fewer off street parking spaces in relation to the floor area than a movie theater would.

IX. Nonconforming Uses

Since zoning is not retroactive, all zoning ordinances must contain a provision for nonconforming uses. If a use has already been established within a particular district before adoption of the ordinance, it must be permitted to continue. Provisions are, however, put into

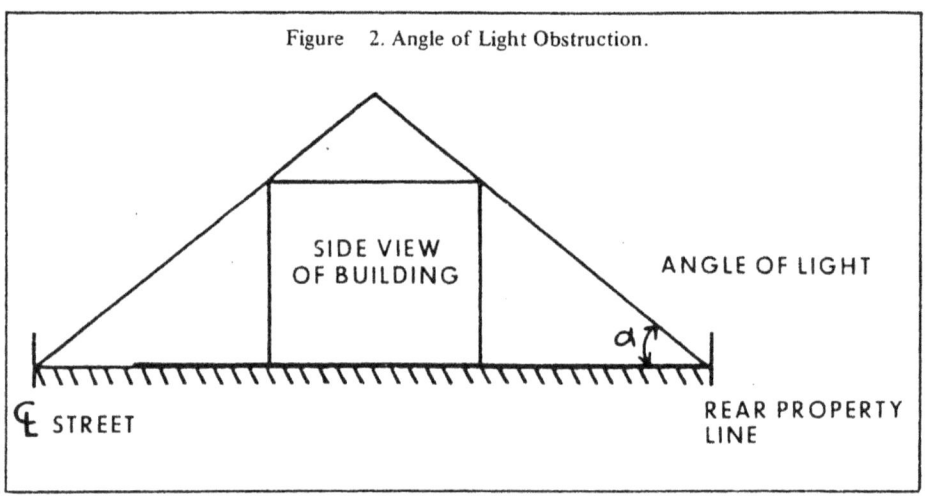

Figure 2. Angle of Light Obstruction.

The ordinance to aid in eliminating nonconforming use. These provisions generally prohibit the following: (1) An enlargement or expansion of the nonconforming uses, (2) reconstruction of the nonconforming use if more than a certain portion is destroyed, (3) resumption of the use after it has been abandoned for a period of specified time, and (4) changing the use to a higher classification or to another nonconforming use. Some zoning ordinances further provide a period of amortization during which the nonconforming land use must be phased out.

X. Variances

Zoning ordinances contain provisions for permitting variances and providing a method of granting these variances subject to certain specified conditions. A variance may be granted when, owing to a particular lot shape, topography, or other lot characteristics, an undue hardship would be imposed on the owner if the exact content of the ordinance is adhered to. For example, assume we have a piece of irregularly shaped property located in a district having the side yard requirements of 20 feet on a side and total lot size requirement of 10,000 square feet. Suppose that our property contains 10,200 feet and thus meets the area requirements; however, let us further assume that, owing to the irregular shape of the property, we can provide side yards of only 15 feet on a side. Since a hardship would be imposed if the exact letter of the law is held to, the zoning board of adjustment could be asked for a variance. Since there is sufficient total open area and since a lessening of the ordinance is not detrimental to the surrounding property, a variance would probably be granted.

Before a variance can be granted, it must be shown that (1) there is a practical hardship, (2) that the variance is needed for the owner to realize a reasonable return on the property, (3) that the original intent of the ordinance will be adhered to, (4) that the character of the neighborhood will not be changed, and (5) that the public's safety and welfare will be preserved.

XI. Exceptions

An exception is often confused with a variance. In every city there are some necessary uses that do not correspond to the permitted land uses within the district. The zoning code recognizes, however, that if proper safeguards were to be provided, these uses would not have a detrimental effect on the district. An example would be a fire substation, which could be permitted in a residential area provided the station house is designed to resemble a residential dwelling and further provided the property is properly landscaped.

XII. Administration

The key man in the zoning process is the zoning inspector, since he must come in contact with each case. In many cases the zoning inspector may also be the building inspector or the housing inspector. Since the building inspector or housing inspector is already in the field making inspections, it is relatively easy for him to check compliance with a zoning ordinance. This compliance can be checked by comparing the actual land use against that allowed for the area and shown on the zoning map.

Each zoning ordinance has a map as a part of the ordinance giving the permitted usage for each block. By taking a copy of this map with him, the inspector can make a preliminary check of the land use in the field. If the use does not conform, the inspector must then check with the Zoning Board to see if the property in question was a "nonconforming use" at the time of passage of the ordinance and if an exception has been granted. In cities where up-to-date records of existing nonconforming uses and exceptions granted are maintained, the inspector can check the use in the field against the records.

When violation is observed and the property owner is duly notified of the violation, he then has the right of hearing before a Zoning Board of Adjustment (sometimes also called the Zoning Board of Appeals). The Board may uphold the zoning enforcement officer or may rule in favor of the property owner. If the action of the zoning enforcement officer is upheld, the property owner may, if he so desires, seek relief through the courts; otherwise the violation will be corrected to conform to the zoning code.

XIII. How Zoning Can Benefit the Housing Inspector

It is of critical importance for the housing inspector, the building inspector, and the zoning inspector to work closely together in cities where these positions and responsibilities are separate. Experience has shown that when illegal conversions or uses of properties occur, these illegally converted properties are often among the most substandard encountered in the city and often contain especially dangerous housing code violations.

In communities where the zoning code is enforced effectively, the resulting zoning compliance in new and existing housing helps advance, as well as sustain, many of the minimum standards of the housing code such as occupancy, ventilation, light, and unimpeded egress. By the same token, building or housing inspectors can often aid the zoning inspector by helping eliminate some nonconforming uses through code enforcement.

XIV. Example of Zoning and Housing Relationships

The following cases will illustrate these relationships:

A Case 1

Two and one-half-story, 13-room house. Originally it had these features:

a   Five-room dwelling unit on first floor including a three-piece bathroom.

b   Eight-room dwelling unit occupying the second and third floors including one bathroom of three pieces on the second floor. The second and third floors are served by only one staircase.

c   Two oil burners, one heating first floor, the other the second and third floors.

It is located in a residential zoning district where two-family housing is the maximum use permitted.

Five years later, while making a regular inspection, the zoning officer found this house in the process of being converted into a three-family use in violation of the zoning ordinance. The owner has already done these things.

a   Made second floor into a separate five-room dwelling unit.

b   Started converting the three rooms on the third floor into another apartment by:

1. Installing a three-piece bathroom, 35 square feet in area, against the windowless west wall of the center bedroom, the habitable area being thus reduced to 40 square feet, and setting up the remainder of the area as the living room by providing a coffee table, lamp, and two overstuffed chairs;

2. Putting in a wall kitchenette consisting of a sink with cold water and a stove, plus a table, lamp, and cupboards in the rear bedroom that is 60 square feet in area;

3. Equipping the front bedroom that is 90 square feet in size with two beds, chest of drawers, and other bedroom furnishings for two.

He admitted, however, that he had not checked on state tenement house law requirements since he did not realize multiple dwellings of three families or more are covered by this law.

Question: How many violations (either housing or zoning) can you find?

Answer: As a result of these actions by the owner, the house now has one more dwelling unit than is permitted by the zoning ordinance in this residential district and also contains these obvious housing code violations:

(a) Threatened over occupancy of the third-floor dwelling unit (only 190 square feet available, but 250 square feet habitable floor space is the minimum required for two occupants).

(b) Size of the front bedroom inadequate by 30 square feet if it is used by two occupants. The back bedroom lacks the requirements needed for occupancy by one person (70 square feet). If a third person lived in the dwelling unit the minimum required habitable floor area would then become 350 square feet.

(c) The bathroom does not meet the light and ventilation requirements.

(d) The kitchen sink does not have hot water.

(e) No refrigerator is provided.

(f) From the description it sounds as if one might have to go through a sleeping room to reach the bathroom. This would be a violation.

(g) Both the second and third floor units are in violation since they lack two means of egress.

B Case 2

Assume that a three-family dwelling unit is the largest size permitted in the zoning district where the building in question is located. The housing inspector's investigation of the three-story dwelling from cellar to roof showed that it contained:

1. Four dwelling units, two with six rooms each and two with three rooms each.

2. Five families, three in separate dwelling units and the two on the third floor in one unit.

3. A bathroom and a kitchen on the second floor shared by two families.

4. The bathroom and kitchen on the third floor also being shared by two families.

5. Inadequate means of egress from the dwelling unit in the third floor.

Question: If you were the housing inspector, what actions would you take?

Answer: In this situation there are definite housing code violations. The housing inspector also knows there is a zoning violation. Because he knows that the property must meet zoning requirements before complying with the housing code, the inspector would refer this case to the zoning department for action.

The housing inspector should never speak for the zoning department and tell the owner that he is in violation of a zoning ordinance unless he and the zoning inspector are the same individual. The housing inspector should complete his housing inspection and leave. Responsibility for informing the owner of any zoning violation lies with the zoning department.

In this particular case, some housing code violations will be corrected through enforcement of zoning. However, there are still violations of requirements for egress, a third kitchen, and a third bathroom.

After compliance with the zoning ordinance has been obtained, the zoning department should notify the housing inspector so that he can then enforce any housing violations that may still exist.

C Case 3

Mr. Jones, a zoning inspector, gets a report that at 1212 Oak Street the owner, Mr. Smith, is converting his single-family house into two apartments and has already started alterations. Investigations of the zoning map shows that in this district, apartments, up to four, are permitted if 1,500 square feet of open land area is provided for each apartment. Mr. Jones checks and finds that no building permit has been issued. A site investigation reveals that Mr. Smith has only 2,000 square feet of open area available. He then informs Mr. Smith that he is in violation of the zoning ordinance.

Mr. Smith then appeals to the Zoning Board of Adjustment for a variance to allow him to have two apartments even though he does not have the required 3,000 square feet 0 f open area. His appeal is denied by the board since no real hardship exists. As a result, Mr. Smith must rent the property as a single-family dwelling and is unable to recover the money he has already spent in starting alterations.

Discuss:

1. The actions of Mr. Jones.

Answer: Mr. Jones was justified in citing Mr. Smith for a zoning violation since the proposed open area would have been inadequate.

2 The action of the Board of Adjustment.

Answer: The Board of Adjustment was also justified in upholding the zoning regulations. If the board had not acted in this manner, the crowding on this property could well have started deterioration in surrounding properties.

3 The action of Mr. Smith.

Answer: Mr. Smith had no legitimate complaint when the Board ruled against him. If he had first sought to obtain a building permit, as required by law, he would have been told that his proposed alterations would not meet zoning regulations and hence would not have suffered a monetary loss.

D Case 4

Mr. Edwards requests a building permit to change a three-story single-family house into a two-family unit. Since two-family units are permitted in this district and he has sufficient open area, the permit is granted.

Six months later, the housing inspector, while making a systematic code enforcement inspection, finds that the converted house now has an apartment on each of the three floors. The bath on the second floor is shared by families on the second and third floors. This is a violation of the housing code.

Knowing that all the other houses on this street are only one- or two-family units, he also suspects a zoning violation. After returning to the office, he contacts the zoning department and learns that Mr. Edwards is in violation of the zoning ordinance as well as of the housing code.

Question: Which ordinance must be enforced first and why?

Answer: The zoning ordinance must be enforced first, since a zoning ordinance is a "primary" ordinance and determines the land use of a particular property. A housing code ordinance is a "secondary" ordinance and sets standards of residential usage on the property.

E   Case 5

During a routine inspection, the housing inspector finds a house with three families, one of which is living in a cellar apartment.

Question: What actions should he take?

Answer: The inspector should immediately cite the owner for a violation of the ordinance and then follow through to see that the situation is corrected. If the family living in the cellar requires housing assistance as a result of corrective measures taken, the housing inspector should inform them of public agencies available for assistance.

F   Case 6

During a routine inspection of a district zoned for up to three-family use, the housing inspector encounters a house that the owner says contains two dwelling units in addition to his own, and also one rooming unit. The inspector finds a cook stove in the "rooming unit."

Question: What actions should he take?

Answer: Although a rooming unit would be permitted in this district, the addition of a cook stove changes the rooming unit into a dwelling unit.

The inspector should refer this case to the zoning department for immediate action and then follow up for housing violations at a later date.

G   Case 7

The housing inspector is investigating a complaint of alleged housing violations. The owner refuses to admit the inspector inside the building and becomes belligerent.

Question: What should the inspector do next?

Answer: The inspector should remain courteous and not lose his temper. If the inspector is not able to obtain permission to inspect without further arousing the owner, he should leave.

Since recent decisions of the U.S. Supreme Court have dictated the inclusion of requirements to obtain a search warrant in cases where entry to the inspector is denied, the inspector should obtain a warrant. He will then return at a later time with someone to serve the warrant.

H   Case 8

During an inspection in July, the housing inspector finds a house that has been converted into two apartments. While checking the basement, he sees that the furnace appears in an unsafe condition. Further checking reveals that there is no provision for heat in the second apartment.

Question: What action should the inspector take since it is July and heat is not now needed. Besides, how does he know that the owner will not install heat before winter?

Answer: The inspector should cite the owner for a violation of the housing code anyway. In his notice of violations, because it is July, he can give the owner sufficient time to comply. He would also send a copy of the letter to the heating inspector for follow up.

I   Case 9

During an inspection, the housing inspector is greeted at the door by a 10-year-old boy who is alone. The boy says it is all right to make the inspection.

Question: Should he? Why?

Answer: No. Permission to enter must be obtained from a responsible adult. Suppose that instead of the 10-year-old boy, he had found a 16-year-old girl.

Question: How would these change things? Why?

Answer: It would not change things, since the 16-year-old girl is not considered a responsible adult. For the protection of the inspector, some housing departments would not permit him to enter alone when the house is occupied by only a female, especially one under age.

J   Case 10

During his inspections the housing inspector finds a house that has no bathroom but does have an outside pit privy.

Question: What action should be taken?

Answer: The inspector should issue a violation for lack of indoor toilet facilities and follow through the regular steps established. by his housing department. A copy of the violation should also be sent to the health department for any actions that they may wish to take for elimination of the privy.

K   Case 11

A number of violations are found in a residence, but the family is occupying the unit under a land purchase contract agreement with the landlord. The owner holds title until enough rent is paid to equal the sale price. The repairs needed are more than the family can afford and are such that the building should be declared unfit for occupancy. The family now has $2,000 worth of equity in the property.

Questions: What actions should the inspector take? Who is responsible for repairs? Who will lose money?

Answer: The inspector would cite the owner of record for a housing violation, since the owner of record is responsible for repairs. If the owner will not bring the building into compliance with the code, the building should be posted as unfit for habitation and the family removed.

The family buying will probably lose in this situation. Before contracting to buy, they should have obtained a certificate of inspection from the housing department showing any violations existing at the time of purchase.

L   Case 12

The property at 112 East Street is owned by an out-of-state individual. The housing inspector found the property unfit for habitation and has had the family renting the property removed. The house is now vacant and the out-of-town owners will not make the repairs since the cost of the necessary

repairs would be too great in relation to the value of the property. The property is in an area that will probably be included in a future urban renewal project within the next few years.

Complaints have been made to the housing department by the neighbors that the house has its windows broken out and its doors broken open. Children play inside during the day and have almost set the building on fire several times. Moreover, vagrants occasionally sleep inside at night.

Question: What action would you take if you were the housing inspector?

Answer: After following standard department procedures, the housing inspector should recommend, that the house be demolished and this cost assessed as a lien against the property. If allowed to remain, the house will be a detriment to surrounding properties and also to the neighborhood.

M   Case 13

During a routine inspection, you find a house with very poor premises sanitation and evidence of roaches, flies, and rats. The property meets minimum housing standards otherwise.

Question: What action can you take?

Answer: The action depends on local regulations and procedures. In many communities the housing program is organizationally located within the health department. In that case, the housing inspector would probably follow through in requiring elimination of the infestation. If the housing inspection program were located within a department other than the health department, the housing inspector may refer the case to the health department for action.

N Case 14

While making a systematic code inspection, the housing inspector encounters a lady who questions the inspector regarding his findings on the house next door, which she is sure is much worse than hers.

Question: How should the inspector deal with the lady?

Answer: The inspector must be very courteous and tactful in his conversation and inform her that he is not permitted to discuss his survey findings for other properties.

BUILDING ASPECTS OF A HOUSING INSPECTION

CONTENTS

		Page
I.	Background Factors	1
II.	Housing Construction Terminology	1
III.	Structure	4
IV.	Discussion of Inspection Techniques	15
V.	Noise as an Environmental Stress	17

BUILDING ASPECTS OF A HOUSING INSPECTION

The principle function of a house is to furnish protection from the elements. In its current stage, however, our civilization requires that a home provide not only shelter but also privacy, safety, and reasonable protection of our physical and mental health. A living facility that fails to offer these essentials through adequately designed and properly maintained interiors and exteriors cannot be termed "healthful housing."

I. Background Factors

In this chapter, a building will be considered in terms of its major components: heating, plumbing, and electrical systems. Each of these items will be examined in detail in future chapters. Attention will be given in this chapter to the portions of a building not visible upon completion of the ceiling, roof, and interior and exterior walls in order to give the reader an understanding of generally accepted construction practices. Emphasis, however, will be placed upon the visible interior and exterior parts of a completed dwelling that have a bearing on the soundness, state of repair, and safety of the dwelling both during intended use and in the event of a fire. These are some of the elements that the housing inspector must examine when making a thorough housing inspection.

II. Housing Construction Terminology

(Key to Component Parts Numbered in Figure 1)

A Fireplace

1 **Chimney** - A vertical masonry shaft of reinforced concrete or other approved noncombustible, heat resisting material enclosing one or more flues. It removes the products of combustion from solid, liquid, or gaseous fuel.

2 **Flue Liner** - The flue is the hole in the chimney. The liner, usually of terra cotta, protects the brick from harmful smoke gases.

3 **Chimney Cap** - This top is generally of concrete. It protects the brick from weather.

4 **Chimney Flashing** - Sheet-metal flashing provides a tight joint between chimney and roof.

5 **Firebrick** - An ordinary brick cannot withstand the heat of direct fire, and so special firebrick is used to line the fireplace.

6 **Ash Dump** - A trap door to let the ashes drop to a pit below, from where they may be easily removed.

7 **Cleanout Door** - The door to the ash pit or the bottom of a chimney through which the chimney can be cleaned.

8 **Chimney Breast** - The inside face or front of a fireplace chimney.

9 **Hearth** - The floor of a fireplace that extends into the room for safety purposes.

B Roof

10 **Ridge** - The top intersection of two opposite adjoining roof surfaces.

11 **Ridge Board** - The board that follows along under the ridge.

12 **Roof Rafters** - The structural members that support the roof.

13 **Collar Beam** - Really not a beam at all. A tie that keeps the roof from spreading. Connects similar rafters on opposite side of roof.

14 **Roof Insulation** - An insulating material (usually rock wool or fiberglas) in a blanket form placed between the roof rafters for the purpose of keeping a house warm in the winter, cool in the summer.

15 **Roof Sheathing** - The boards that provide the base for the finished roof.

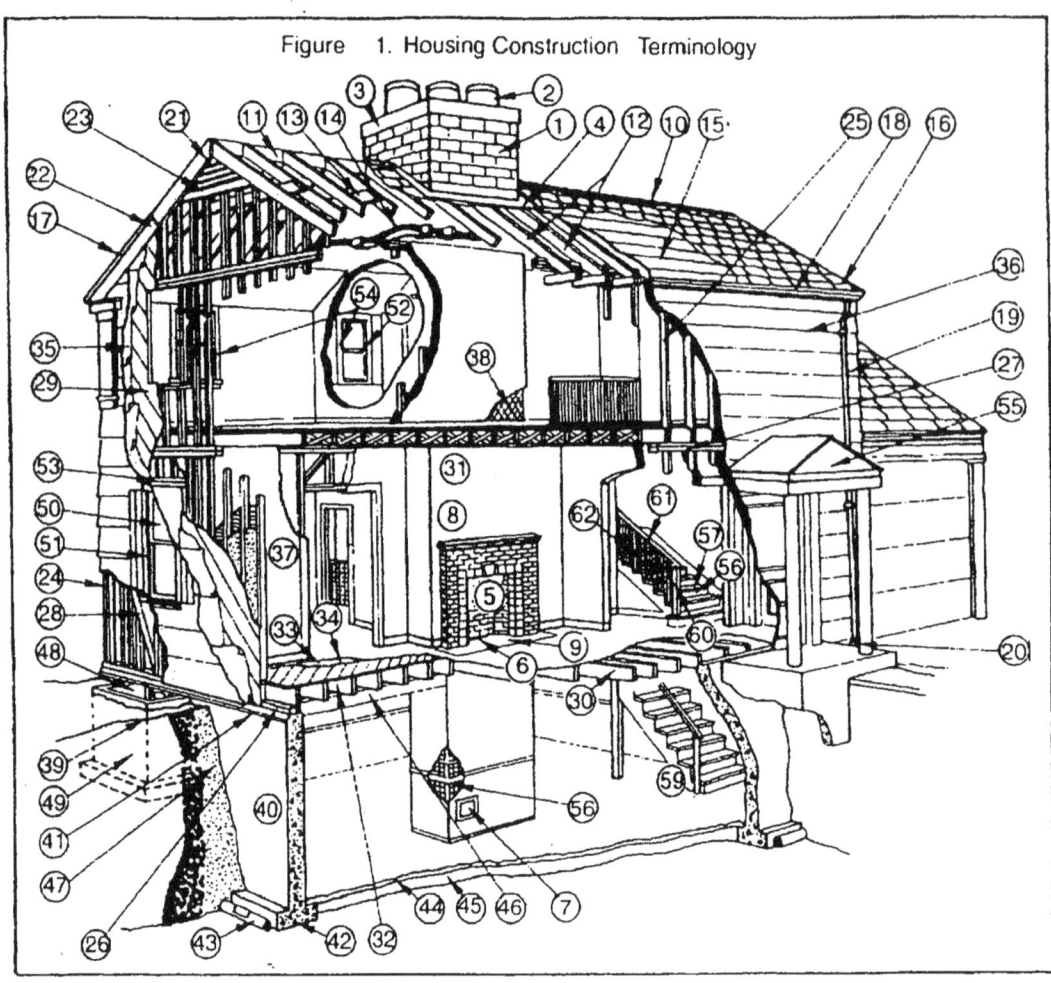

Figure 1. Housing Construction Terminology

    16   **Roofing** - The wood, asphalt, or asbestos shingles - or tile, slate or metal - that form the outer protection against the weather.

    17   **Cornice** - A decorative element made up of molded members usually placed at or near the top of an exterior or interior wall.

    18   **Gutter** - The trough that gathers rainwater from a roof.

    19   **Downspouts** - The pipe that leads the water down from the gutter.

    20   **Storm Sewer Tile** - The underground pipe that receives the water from the downspouts and carries it to the sewer.

    21   **Gable** - The triangular end of a building with a sloping roof.

    22   **Barage Board** - The fascia or board at the gable just under the edge of the roof.

    23   **Louvers** - A series of slanted slots arranged to keep out rain, yet allow ventilation.

C   Walls and Floors

    24   **Corner Post** - The vertical member at the corner of the frame, made up to receive inner and outer covering materials.

    25   **Studs** - The vertical wood members of the house, usually 2 X 4's generally spaced every 16 inches.

    26   **Sill** - The board that is laid first on the foundation, and on which the frame rests.

    27   **Plate** - The board laid across the top ends of the studs to hold them even and rigid.

28   **Corner Bracing** - Diagonal strips to keep the frame square and plumb.

29   **Sheathing** - The first layer of outer wall covering nailed to the studs.

30   **Joist** - The structural members or beams that hold up the floor or ceiling, usually 2 X 10's or 2 X 12's spaced 16 inches apart.

31   **Bridging** - Cross bridging or solid. Members at the middle or third points of joist spans to brace one to the next and to prevent their twisting.

32   **Subflooring** - The rough boards that are laid over the joist. Usually laid diagonally.

33   **Flooring Paper** - A felt paper laid on the rough floor to stop air infiltration and, to some extent, noise.

34   **Finish Flooring** - Usually hardwood, of tongued and grooved strips.

35   **Building Paper** - Paper placed outside the sheathing, not as a vapor barrier, but to prevent water and air from leaking in. Building paper is also used as a tarred felt under shingles or siding to keep out moisture or wind.

36   **Beveled Siding** - Sometimes called clapboards, with a thick butt and a thin upper edge lapped to shed water.

37   **Wall Insulation** - A blanket of wool or reflective foil placed inside the walls.

38   **Metal Lath** - A mesh made from sheet metal onto which plaster is applied.

D   **Foundation and Basement**

39   **Finished Grade Line** - The top of the ground at the foundation.

40   **Foundation Wall** - The wall of poured concrete (shown) or concrete blocks that rests on the footing and supports the remainder of the house.

41   **Termite Shield** - A metal baffle to prevent termites from entering the frame.

42   **Footing** - The concrete pad that carries the entire weight of the house upon the earth.

43   **Footing Drain Tile** - A pipe with cracks at the joints to allow underground water to drain in and away before it gets into the basement.

44   **Basement Floor Slab** - The 4- or 5-inch layer of concrete that forms the basement floor.

45   **Gravel Fill** - Placed under the slab to allow drainage and to guard against a damp floor.

46   **Girder** - A main beam upon which floor joists rest. Usually of steel, but also of wood.

47   **Backfill** - Earth, once dug out, that has been replaced and tamped down around the foundation.

48   **Areaway** - An open space to allow light and air to a window. Also called a light well.

49   **Area Wall** - The wall, of metal or concrete, that forms the open area.

E   **Windows and Doors**

50   **Window** - An opening in a building for admitting light and air. It usually has a pane or panes of glass and is set in a frame or sash that is generally movable for opening and shutting.

51   **Window Frame** - The lining of the window opening.

52 **Window Sash** - The inner frame, usually movable, that holds the glass.

53 **Lintel** - The structural beam over a window or door opening.

54 **Window Casing** - The decorative strips surrounding a window opening on the inside.

F Stairs and Entry

55 **Entrance Canopy** - A roof extending over the entrance door.

56 **Furring** - Falsework or framework necessary to bring the outer surface to where we want it.

57 **Stair Tread** - The horizontal strip where we put our foot when we climb up or down the stairs.

58 **Stair Riser** - The vertical board connecting one tread to the next.

59 **Stair Stringer** - The sloping board that supports the ends of the steps.

60 **Newel** - The post that terminates the railing.

61 **Stair Rail** - The bar used for a handhold when we use the stairs.

62 **Balusters** - Vertical rods or spindles supporting a rail.

III. Structure

A Foundation

The word **foundation** is used to mean:
1. Construction below grade such as footings, cellar or basement walls.
2. The composition of the earth on which the building rests.
3. Special construction such as pilings and piers used to support the building.

The foundation bed may be composed of solid rock, sand, gravel, or unconsolidated sand or clay. Rock, sand, or gravel are the most reliable foundation materials. Unconsolidated sand and clay, though found in many sections of the country, are not as desirable, because they are subject to sliding and settling.

The footing (see Figure 2) distributes the weight of the building over a sufficient area of ground so as to ensure that the foundation walls will stand properly. Footings are usually constructed of a masonry-type material such as concrete; however, in the past wood and stone have been used. Some older houses have been constructed without footings.

Although it is usually difficult to determine the condition of a footing without excavating the foundation, a footing in a state of disrepair or lack of a footing will usually be indicated either by large

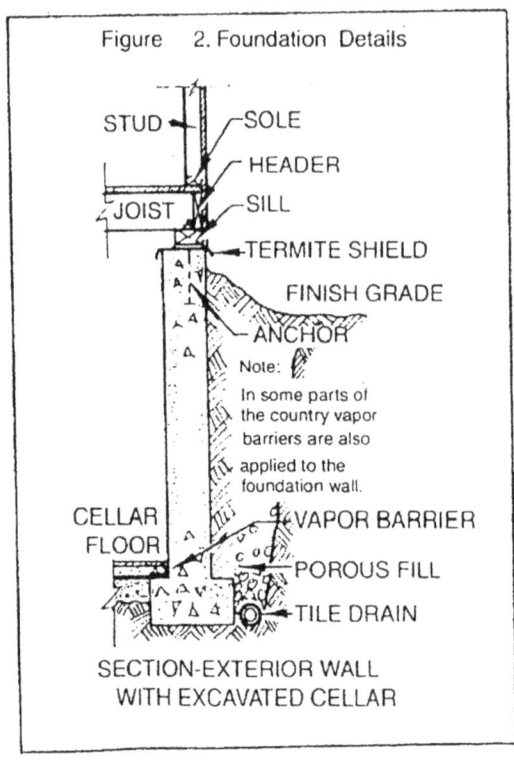

Figure 2. Foundation Details
SECTION-EXTERIOR WALL WITH EXCAVATED CELLAR

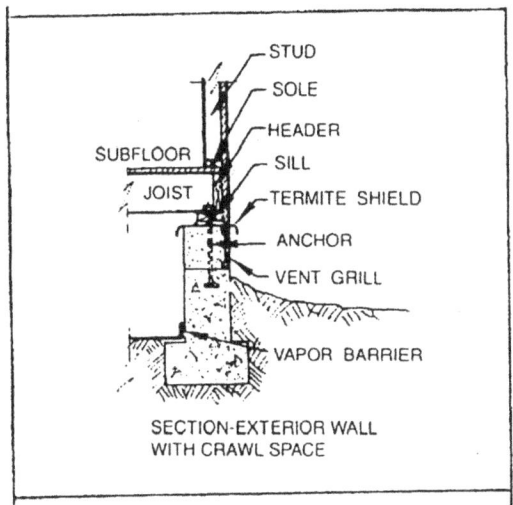

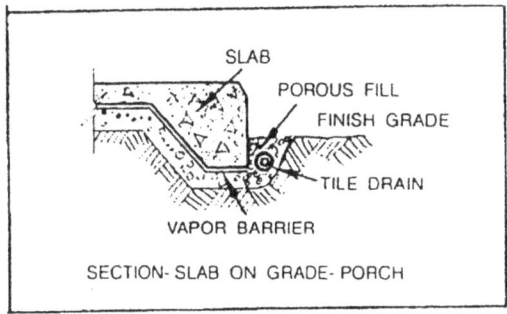

cracks or by settlement in the foundation walls (see Figure 3).

Foundation wall cracks are usually diagonal, starting from the top, the bottom; or the end of the wall. Cracks that do not extend to at least one edge of the wall may not be caused by foundation problems. Such wall cracks may be due to other structural problems and should also be reported.

The foundation walls support the weight of the structure and transfer this weight to the footings. The foundation walls may be made of stone, brick, concrete, or concrete blocks and should be moisture proofed with either a membrane of water-proof material or a coating of portland cement mortar. The membrane may consist of plastic sheeting or a sandwich of standard roofing felt joined and covered with tar or asphalt. The purpose of waterproofing the foundation walls is to prevent water from penetrating the wall material and leaving the basement or cellar walls damp.

Holes in the foundation walls are a common finding in many old houses. These holes may be caused by missing bricks or blocks. Holes and cracks in a foundation wall are undesirable because they make a convenient entry for rats and other rodents and also indicate the possibility of further structural deterioration. These holes should not be confused with adequately installed vents in the foundation wall that permit ventilation and prevent moisture entrapment.

The basement or cellar floor should be made of concrete placed on at least 6 inches of gravel. The purpose of a concrete floor is to protect the basement or cellar from invasion by rodents or from flooding. The gravel distributes ground water movements under the concrete floor, reducing the possibility of the water's penetrating the floor. A waterproof membrane, such as plastic sheeting, should be laid before the concrete is placed for additional protection against flooding.

The basement or cellar floor should be gradually but uniformly sloped towards a drain or a series of drains from all directions. These drains permit the basement or cellar floor to be drained if it becomes flooded.

Evidence of ineffective waterproofing or moisture proofing will be indicated by water or moisture marks on the floor and walls.

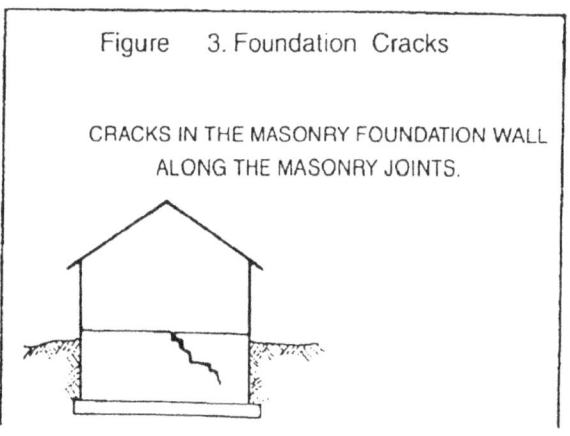

Figure 3. Foundation Cracks

CRACKS IN THE MASONRY FOUNDATION WALL ALONG THE MASONRY JOINTS.

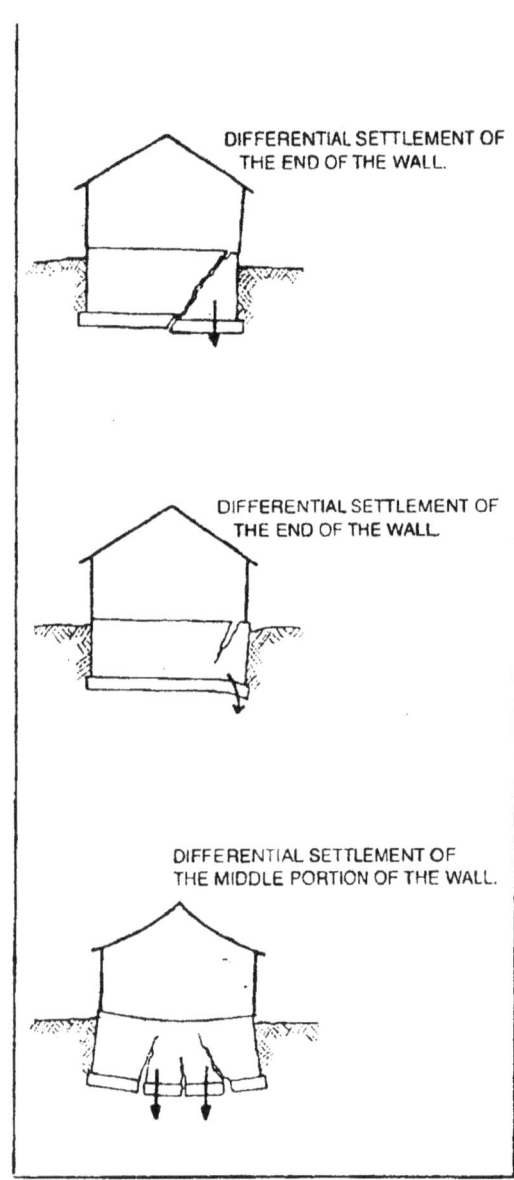

Cellar doors, hatchways, and basement windows should be weathertight and rodent proof. A hatchway can be inspected by standing at the lower portion with the doors closed; if daylight can be seen, the door probably needs repair.

B Framing

Many different types of house-framing systems are found in various sections of the country; however, the majority of the members in each framing system are the same. They include:

1. **Foundation Sills:** (see Figure 4 and 5). The purpose of the sill is to provide support or a bearing surface for the outside walls of the building. The sill is the first part of the frame to be placed and rests directly on the foundation wall. It is bolted to the foundation wall by sill anchors. It is good practice to protect the sill against termites by extending the foundation wall to at least 18 inches above the ground and using a non-corroding metal shield continuously around the outside top of the foundation wall.

2. **Flooring Systems:** (see Figure 5). The flooring system is composed of a combination of girders, joists, sub-flooring, and finished flooring that may be made up of concrete, steel, or wood. Joists are laid perpendicular to the girders, at about 16 inches on centers, and are the members to which the sub-flooring is attached. When the subfloor is wood, it may be nailed at either right angles or diagonally to the joists.

   As shown in Figure 5, a girder is a member that in certain framing systems supports the joists and is usually a larger section than the joists it supports. Girders are found in framing systems where there are no interior bearing walls or where the span between bearing walls is greater than the joists are capable of spanning. The most common application of a girder is to support the first floor in residences. Often a board known as a ledger is applied to the side of a wood girder or beam to form a ledge for the joists to rest upon. The girder, in turn, is supported by wood posts or steel "lally columns" which extend from the cellar or basement floor to the girder.

3. **Studs:** (see Figure 4 and 5). Wall studs are almost always 2 by 4

inches; studs 2 by 6 inches are occasionally used to provide a wall thick enough to permit the passage of waste pipes. There are two types of walls or partitions: bearing and nonbearing. A bearing wall is constructed at right angles to and supports the joists. A nonbearing wall or partition acts as a screen or enclosure; hence, the headers in it are often parallel to the joists of the floor above.

In general, studs like joists are spaced 16 inches on center. In light construction such as garages and summer cottages where plaster is omitted, or some other material is used for a wall finish, wider spacing on studs is common.

Openings for windows or doors must be framed in studs. This framing consists of horizontal members called "headers," and vertical members called "trimmers" (see Figure 1).

Since the vertical spaces between studs can act as flues to transmit flames in the event of a fire, "fire stops" are important in preventing or retarding fire from spreading through a building by way of air passages in walls, floors, and partitions. Fire stops are wood obstructions placed between studs or floor joists to prevent fire from spreading in these natural fluespaces.

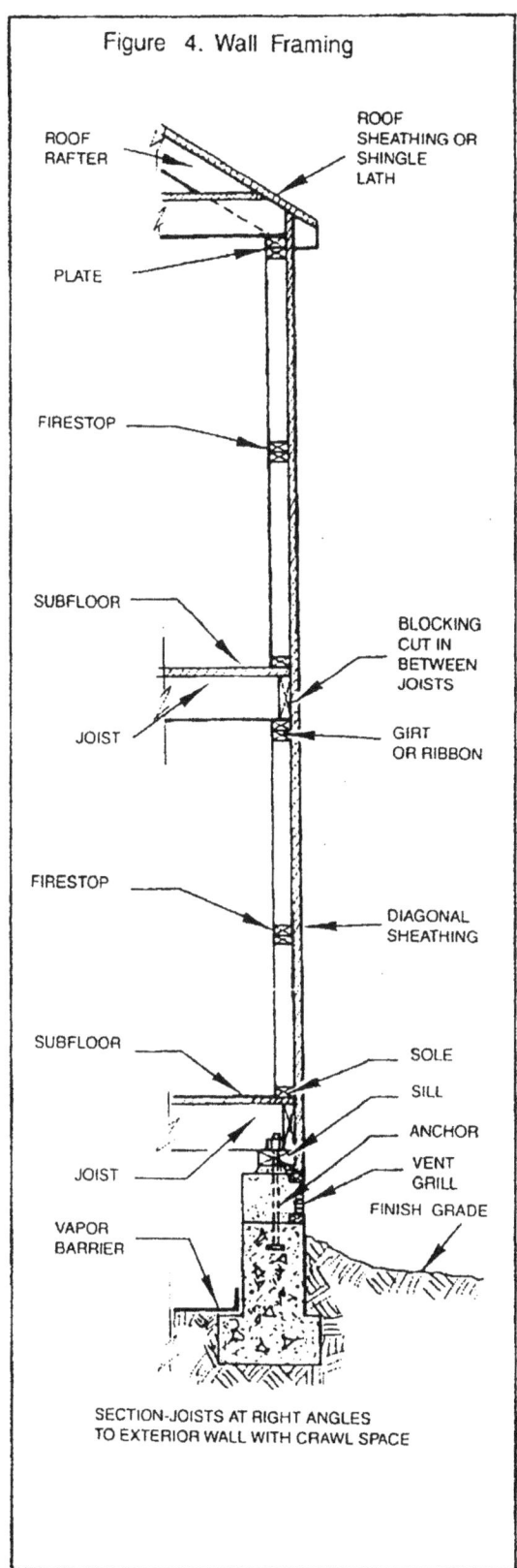

Figure 4. Wall Framing

4 **Interior Wall Finish:** Many types of materials are used for covering interior walls and ceilings, but the principal types are plaster and dry-wall construction. Plaster is a mixture, usually lime, sand, and water, applied in two or three coats to lath to form a hard-wall surface. Dry-wall finish is a material that requires little, if any, water for application. More specifically, dry-wall finish may be gypsum board, plywood, fiberboard, or wood in various sizes and forms.

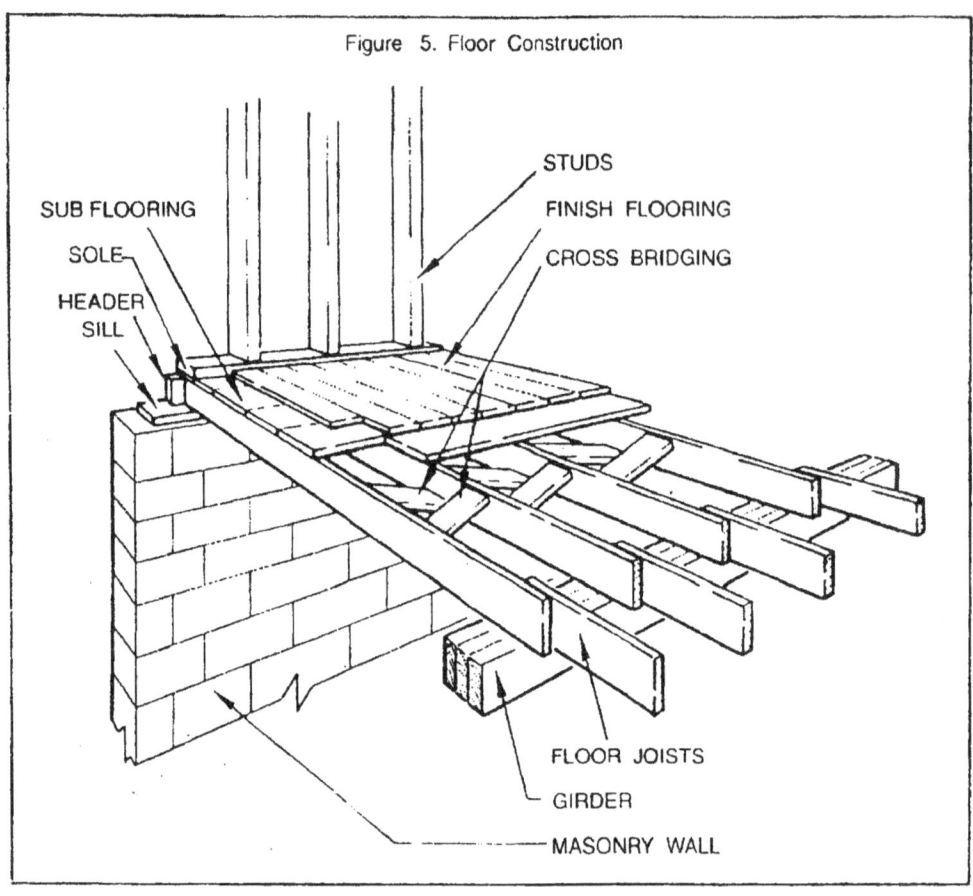

Figure 5. Floor Construction

Gypsum board is a sheet material composed of a gypsum filler faced with paper. Sheets are usually 4 feet wide and can be obtained in lengths up to 12 feet. In dry-wall construction, gypsum boards are fastened to the studs either vertically or horizontally and then painted. The edges along the length of the sheet are recessed to receive joint cement and tape.

A plaster finish requires a base upon which plaster can be spread. Wood lath at one time was the plaster base most commonly used, but today gypsum-board lath is more popular. It has paper faces with a gypsum filler. Such lath is 16 by 48 inches and 1/2 or 3/8 inches thick.

It is applied horizontally across the studs. Gypsum lath may be perforated to improve the bond and thus lengthen the time the plaster can remain intact when exposed to fire. The building codes in some cities require that gypsum lath be perforated. Expanded-metal lath may also be used as a plaster base. Expanded-metal lath consists of sheet metal slit and expanded to form openings to hold the plaster. Metal lath is usually 27 by 96 inches and is fastened to the studs.

Plaster is applied over the base to a minimum thickness of 1/2 inch. Because some drying may take place in wood-framing members after the house is completed, some shrinkage can be expected, which, in turn, may cause plaster cracks to develop around openings and in corners. Strips of lath imbedded in the plaster at these locations prevent cracks.

On the inside face of studs that form an exterior wall, vapor barriers are used to prevent condensation on the wall. The vapor barrier is an asphalted paper or metal foil through which moisture-laden air cannot travel.

5 **Stairways:** (see Figure 6). The general purpose of the standards for stairway dimensions is to ensure that there is adequate headroom, width, and uniformity in riser and tread size of every step to accommodate the expected traffic on each stairway safely.

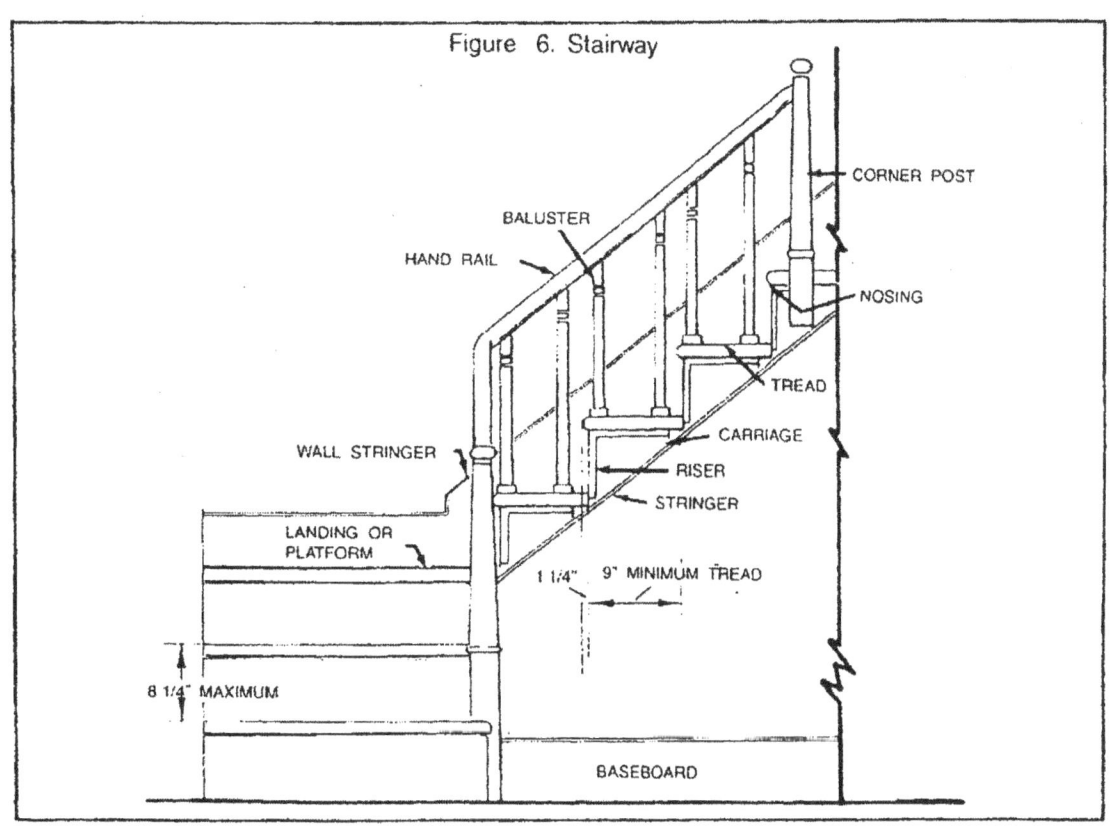

Figure 6. Stairway

Interior stairways should be not less than 44 inches in width. The width of a stairway may be reduced to 36 inches in one- and two-family dwellings. Stairs with closed risers should have maximum risers of 8 1/4 inches and a minimum tread of 9 inches plus 1 1/4-inch nosing. Basement stairs are often constructed with open risers. These stairs should have maximum risers of 8 1/4 inches and minimum treads of 9 inches plus 1/2-inch nosing. The headroom in all parts of the stair enclosure should be no less than 80 inches.

Exterior stairway dimensions should be the same as those called for in interior stairways, except that the headroom requirement does not apply.

6 **Windows:** The four general classifications of windows for residences are:

a Double-hung sash window that moves up or down, balanced by weights hung on chains or ropes, or springs on each side.

b Casement window sash is hinged at the side and can be hung so that it will swing outward or inward.

c Awning window - usually has two or more glass panes that are hinged at the top and swing about a horizontal axis.

d Sliding window - usually has two or more glass panes that slide past one another on a horizontal track.

The principal parts of a double-hung window (see Figure 4-7) are the lights, the top rail-framing members, bars or muntins that separate the lights, stiles - side-framing members, bottom rail, sash weights, and sash cords or chains. (All rails are horizontal, all stiles vertical.) The casement window's principal parts include: top and bottom rails, muntins, butt hinges, and jamb. All types of windows should open freely and close securely.

The exterior sill is the bottom projection of a window. The drip cap is a separate piece of wood projecting over the top of the window and is a component of the window casing.

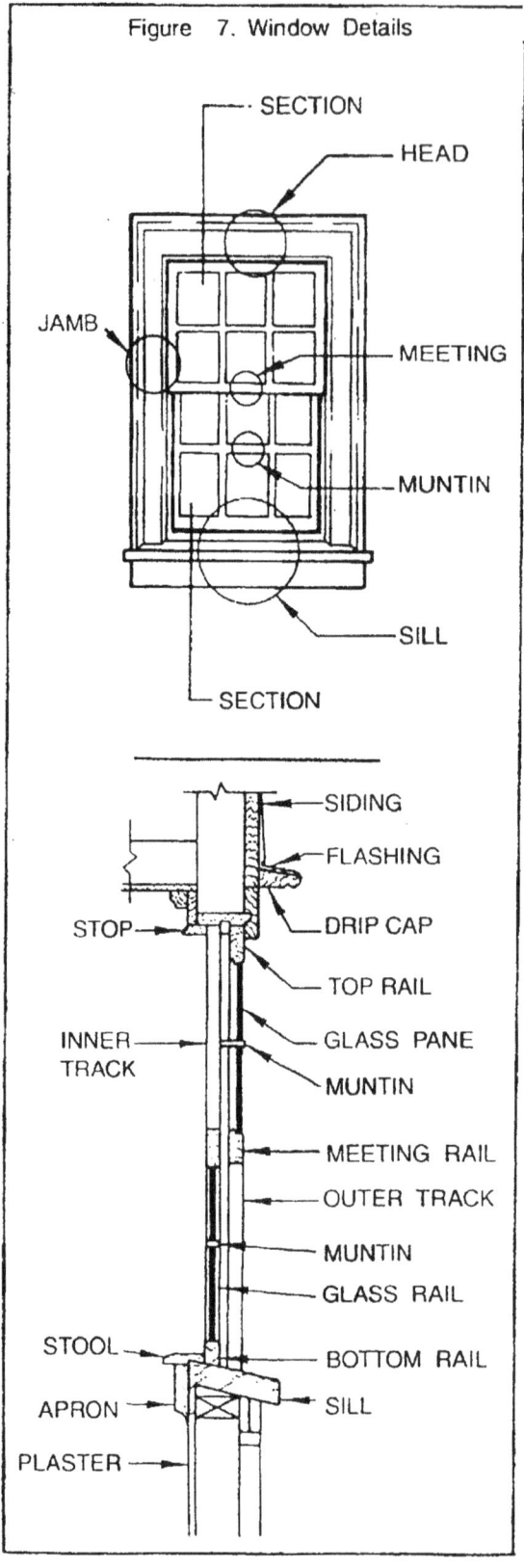

Figure 7. Window Details

7 **Doors:** There are many styles of doors both for exterior and interior use. Interior doors should offer a rea-

sonable degree of privacy. Exterior doors must, in addition to offering privacy, protect the interior of the structure from the elements. The various parts of a door have the same definitions as the corresponding parts of a window.

The most common types of doors are:

a **Batten door**: This consists of boards nailed together in various ways. The simplest is two layers nailed to each other at right angles, usually with each layer at 45 degrees to the vertical.

Another type of batten door consists of vertical boards nailed at right angles to several (two to four) cross strips called ledgers, with diagonal bracing members nailed between ledgers. If vertical members corresponding to ledgers are added at the sides, the verticals are called frames.

Batten doors are often found in cellars and other places where appearance is not a factor and economy is desired.

b **Flush doors**: Solid flush doors are perfectly flat, usually on both sides, although occasionally they are made flush on one side and paneled on the other. Flush doors sometimes are solid planking, but they are commonly veneered and possess a core of small pieces of white pine or other wood. These pieces are glued together with staggered end joints. Along the sides, top, and bottom are glued 3/4-inch edge strips of the same wood, used to create a smooth surface that can be cut or planed. The front and back faces are then covered with a 1/8-to 1/4-inch layer of veneer.

Solid flush doors may be used on both the interior and exterior.

c **Hollow-core doors**: These, like solid flush doors, are perfectly flat, but unlike solid doors, the core consists mainly of a grid of crossed wooden slats or some other type of grid construction. Faces are 3-ply plywood instead of one or two plies of veneer, and the surface veneer may be any species of wood, usually hardwood. The edges of the core are solid wood and are made wide enough at the appropriate places to accommodate locks and butts. Doors of this kind are considerably lighter than solid flush doors.

Hollow-core doors are usually used as interior doors.

d **Paneled doors**: Most doors are paneled, with most panels consisting of solid wood or plywood, either "raised" or "flat," although exterior doors frequently have one or more panels of glass, in which case they are called "lights." One or more panels may be employed although the number seldom exceeds eight. Paneled doors may be used both on the interior or exterior.

In addition to the various types of wood doors, metal is often used as a veneer or for the frame.

In general, the horizontal members are called rails and the vertical members are called stiles. Every door has a top and bottom rail, and some may have intermediate rails. There are always at least two stiles, one on each side of the door. The frame of a doorway is the portion to which the door is hinged. It consists of two side jambs and a head jamb, with an integral or attached stop against which the door closes.

Exterior door frames are ordinarily of softwood plank, with side rabbitted to receive the door in the same way as casement windows. At the foot is a sill, made of hardwood to withstand the wear of traffic, and sloped down and out to shed water.

Interior door frames are similar to exterior, except that they are often set directly on the hardwood flooring without a sill.

Building codes throughout the country call for doors in various locations within the structure to be fire resistant. These doors are often covered with metal or some other fire-resistant materials, and some are completely constructed of metal. Fire-resistant doors are usually located between a garage and a house, stairwells and hallways, all boiler rooms. The fire resistance rating required for various doors differs with local fire codes

C **Roof Framing** (see Figures 1, 4, 8, and 9)

Rafters serve the same purpose for the roof as joists do for floors, i.e., providing support for sheathing and roofing material. Rafters are usually spaced 20 inches on center.

1 **Collar Beam:** Collar beams are ties between rafters on opposite sides of the roof. If the attic is to be used for rooms, the collar beam may double as the ceiling joist.

2 **Purlin:** A purlin is the horizontal member that forms the support for the rafters at the intersection of the two slopes of a gambrel roof.

3 **Ridge Board:** A ridge board is a horizontal member against which the rafters rest at their upper ends; it forms a lateral tie to make them secure.

4 **Hip:** Like a ridge except that it slopes. The intersection of two adjacent, rather than two opposite, roof planes.

5 **Roof Boards:** The manner in which roof boards are applied depends upon the type of roofing material. Roof boards may vary from tongue-and-groove lumber to plywood panels.

6 **Dormer:** The term dormer window is applied to all windows in the roof of a building, whatever their size and shape.

D **Exterior Walls and Trim** (see Figure 4 and 9)

Exterior walls are enclosure walls whose purpose is to make the building weathertight. In most one- to three-story buildings they also serve as bearing walls. These walls may be made of many different materials.

Frequently used framed exterior walls appear to be of brick construction. In this situation, the brick is only one course thick and is called a brick veneer. It supports nothing but itself and is kept from toppling by ties connected to the frame wall.

In frame construction the base material of the exterior walls is called "sheathing." The sheathing material may be square-edge, shiplap, or tongue-and-groove boards.

In recent construction there has been a strong trend toward the use of plywood or composition panels.

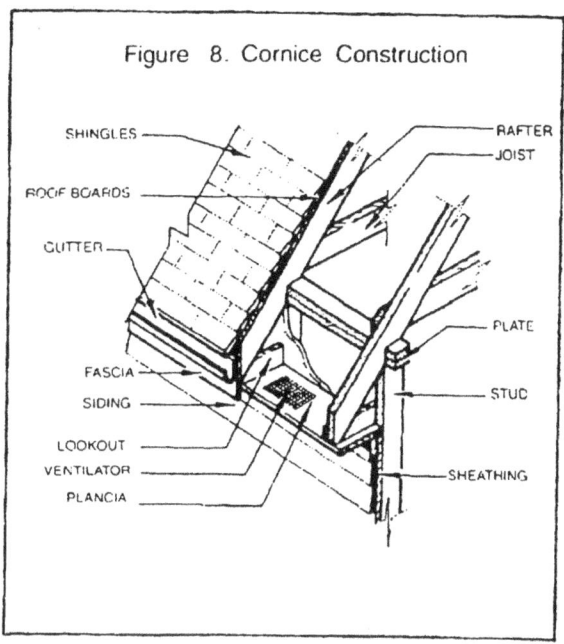

Figure 8. Cornice Construction

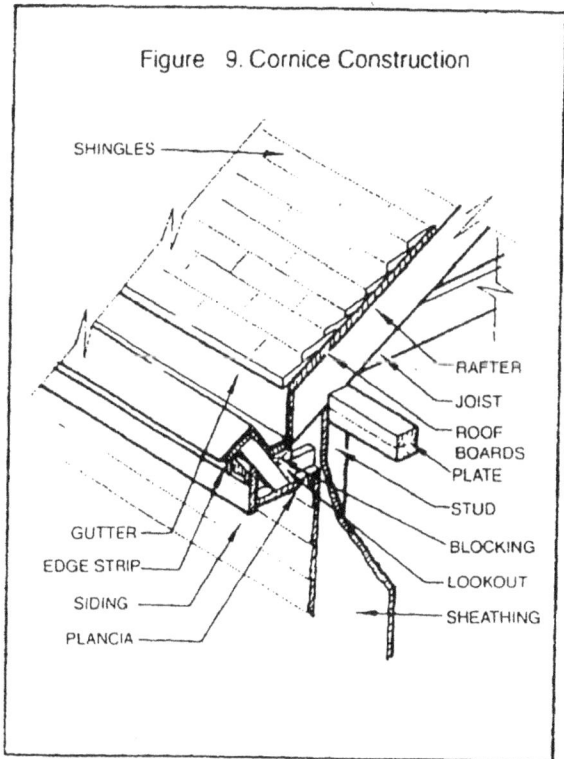

Figure 9. Cornice Construction

Sheathing, in addition to serving as a base course for the finished siding material, stiffens the frame to resist sway caused by wind. It is for this reason that sheathing has been applied diagonally on frame buildings.

The finished siding may be clapboard, shingles, aluminum, brick asphalt, wood, and so forth, or a combination thereof. Good aluminum siding has a backer board that serves as added insulation and affords rigidity to the siding. Projecting cornices are a decorative trim found at the top of the building's roofline. A parapet wall is that part of the masonry wall that extends up and beyond the roofline and is capped with a noncombustible material. It helps prevent spread of fire, provides a rest for fire department ladders, and helps prevent people on the roof from falling off.

Many types of siding, shingles, and other exterior coverings are applied over the sheathing. Wood siding, cedar, and other wood shingles or shakes, clapboard, common siding (called bevel siding), composition siding, asbestos, cement shingles, asbestos-cement siding, and the aforementioned aluminum siding are commonly used for exterior coverings. Clapboards and common siding differ only in the length of the pieces. Clapboards are 4 feet long while panel siding comes in lengths from 6 to 16 feet. Composition siding is made of felt and asphalt, which are often shaped to look like brick. Asbestos and cement shingles are rigid and produce a covering that is fire resistant. Cedar wood shingles are also manufactured with a backer board that gives insulation and fire-resistant qualities. Asbestos cement siding made of asbestos fiber and portland cement has good fire-resistant qualities and is a rigid covering.

E Roof Coverings (Flexible Material Class)

1 **Asphalt Shingle:** The principal damage to asphalt shingle roofs is caused by the action of strong winds on shingles nailed too high. Usually the shingles affected by winds are those in the four or five courses nearest the ridge and in the area

extending about 5 feet down from the edge or rake of the roof.

2. **Asphalt Built-up Roofs:** These may be un-surfaced, the coating of bitumen being exposed directly to the weather, or they may be surfaced having slag or gravel imbedded in the bituminous coating. The use of surfacing material is desirable as a protection against wind damage and the elements. This type of roof should have enough pitch to drain water readily.

3. **Coal Tar Pitch Built-up Roofs:** This type roof must be surfaced with slag or gravel. Coal tar pitch built-up roof should always be used on deck pitched less than 1/2 inch per foot; that is, where waler may collect and stand. This type roof should be inspected on completion, 6 months later, and then at least once a year, preferably in the fall. When the top coating of bitumen shows damage or has become badly weathered, it should be renewed (rigid material class).

4. **Slate Roofs:** The most common problem with slate roofs is the replacement of broken slates. Roofs of this type normally render long service with little or no repair.

5. **Tile Roofs:** Replacement of broken shingle tiles is the main maintenance problem. This is one of the most expensive roofing materials. It requires very little maintenance and gives long service.

6. **Copper Roofs:** Usually are of 16-ounce copper sheeting and applied to permanent structures. When properly installed, they require practically no maintenance or repair. Proper installation allows for expansion and contraction with changes in temperature.

7. **Galvanized Iron Roofs:** Maintenance is done principally by removing rust and keeping roof well painted. Leaks can be corrected by re-nailing, caulking, or replacing all or part of the sheet or sheets in disrepair.

8. **Wood Shingle Roofs:** The most important factors of this type roof are its pitch and exposure, the character of wood, kind of nails used, and preservative treatment given shingles. Creosote and coal tar preservative are satisfactory for both treated and untreated shingles.

9. **Flashing:** Valleys in roofs that are formed by the junction of two downward slopes may be finished, open, or closed. In a closed valley the slates, tiles, or shingles of one side meet those of the other, and the flashing below them may be comparatively narrow. In an open valley, the flashing, which may be made of zinc, copper, or aluminum, is laid in a continuous strip, extending 12 to 18 inches on each side of the valley, while the tiles or slates do not come within 4 to 6 inches of it.

The ridges built up on a sloping roof where it runs down against a vertical projection, like a chimney or a skylight, should be weather-proofed with flashing.

Metal flashings are generally used with slate, tile, metal, and wood shingles. Failure of roof flashing is usually due to exposed nails that have come loose. The loose nails allow the flashing to lift with leakage resulting.

10. **Gutters and Leaders:** Gutters and leaders should be of noncombustible materials. They should be securely fastened to the structure and spill into a storm sewer if the neighborhood is so provided. When there is no storm sewer, a concrete or stone block placed on the ground beneath the leader prevents water from eroding the lawn. This store

block is called a splash block. Gutters will not become plugged if protected against clogging of leaves and twigs. Gutters should be checked every spring and fall and then cleaned out when necessary.

IV. Discussion of Inspection Techniques

A serious building defect may often be observed during a housing inspector's routine examination. In many cases it is beyond the scope of the housing inspector's background to analyze the underlying causes and to recommend a course of action that will facilitate repair in an efficient and economical manner. In situations such as this, it is important that the inspector realize his limitations and refer the matter to the proper expert.

A prime example of a technically complex situation that a housing inspector might observe is a leaning, buckling, or bulging foundation or bearing wall. This problem may be the result of a number of hidden or interacting problems. For example, it may be the result of differential building settlement or failure of a structural beam or girder. It is beyond the scope of the housing inspector's responsibilities to discover the cause of the defect, but it is his responsibility to note the problem and refer it to the proper authority. In this case the proper authority would be a building inspector.

In the aforementioned situation where a bulging foundation wall was discovered, this would obviously constitute a violation of the housing ordinance and should be written up as such by the housing inspector. Since the housing inspector is generally not qualified to determine whether the house should be evacuated because it is in danger of imminent collapse, he should seek the advice of a building inspector.

A question that frequently arises is *which violations should be referred to an expert?* Needless to say, circumstances that obviously fall within the jurisdiction of another department should be referred to the department. The housing inspector should discuss with his supervisor any situation in which he feels inadequate to make a decision. In all cases the inspector should inform his supervisor before referring a problem to another agency or expert.

Another reason for referral to other departments is that when a remedial action is completed the other department will be in a better position to determine whether the job is satisfactory.

This principle of referral should be applied to every portion of the inspection, whether it deals with health, heating, plumbing, gas, or electrical as well as structural defects.

Certain structural items should be recognized as unsafe by the housing inspector. For example, a beam that has sagged or slanted may cause a portion of or an entire floor to sag or slope. Where a sagging or sloping floor is found, examine the ceiling of the room below or the basement for a broken or dropped girder or joist.

Doors and windows that are out of level will not close completely. It may be possible to see outside light through openings around window rails and door jambs. If an inspector detects such a situation, the condition of the supporting girders, girts, posts, and studs should be questioned, since this condition is evidence that some of these members may be termite infested or rotted and may be causing the outside wall to sag. Glass panes in doors and windows should be replaced if found to be broken or missing. Windows should also be checked for proper operation, and items such as broken sash cords or chains noted.

If the roof of the structure appears to be sagging, the inspector should make a special effort to examine the rafters, purlin, collar beams, and ridge boards if these members are exposed as in unfinished attics. The condition of the roof boards may be examined while he is in the attic. If light can be seen between these boards the roof is unsound. Evidence of a leaking roof will be indicated by loose plaster or peeling or stained paint and wall paper. Areas of the roof where flashing occurs, such as around the chimney, are frequent origins of roof leaks. It is essential that the leak be found and repaired, not only to prevent the entrance of moisture into the building, but also to prevent the loosening of the plaster, rotting of timbers, and extension of damage to the remainder of the house.

Gutters and rain leaders should be placed around the entire building to insure proper drainage of water. This will lessen the possibility of seepage of water through siding and window frames, and entrance of water into the cellar or basement. Lack of or leaking gutters may result in rotting of the siding or erosion of the exposed portion of the cellar or basement walls. This situation commonly exists where the mortar between bricks or concrete blocks in foundation walls is found to be heavily eroded. Gutters should be free from dirt and leaves.

The exterior siding should be in sound, weathertight condition. Peeled or worn paint on wood siding will expose the bare wood to the elements and result in splitting and warping of siding. This condition will eventually lead to the entrance of rain water with resultant rotting of the sheathing and studs as well as inside dampness and falling plaster. Sound and painted siding will prevent major repairs and expenses in the future. This condition will often be particularly prevalent on the north face of the structure.

Roof and chimneys should be inspected for tilting, missing bricks, deterioration of flashing, and pointing of chimney bricks. In addition, roof covering should be checked for broken spots and missing shingles or tiles. Roof doors should be metal clad, self-closing, tight fitting, and unlockable. The roof should also be examined for weather-tightness and broken TV antennas.

Porches should be carefully examined for weakened treads, missing or cracked boards, holes, and holes covered with tin plates, railing rigidity, missing posts, handrail rigidity, condition of the columns that support the porch roof, and the condition of the porch roof itself. The open section beneath the porch should be inspected for broken lattice-work. Check under the porch for accumulation of dirt and debris that can offer a harborage for vermin and rodents.

Loose plaster and missing or peeling wallpaper or paint should be noted. Bugs and cockroaches eat the paste from the wallpaper while leaving behind loose paper.

The basic parts of a stairway that a housing inspector should be able to identify correctly are the following:

A   Riser

B   Tread

C   Nosing

D   Handrail

E   Balustrade and Balusters, the Vertical Members that Support the Handrail, and

F   The Soffit, Underpart of the Stairway.

In the examination of a stairway (be careful to turn the light on) initially check the underside, if visible, to see if it is intact. Then proceed slowly up the stairs placing full weight on each tread and checking for loose, wobbling, or uneven treads and risers. Regardless of the size of the treads or risers they should all be of uniform size. For all stairs that rise 3 or more feet, a handrail should be present and in a sound and rigid condition.

Any fireplace should conform to the requirements of the local code. An unused fireplace that has its opening covered with wallpaper or other material should have a solid seal behind the paper. Operable fireplaces should have a workable damper and a fire screen, and should be clean.

Garages and accessory structures should be inspected in the same manner as the main building.

Sidewalks and driveways, whether constructed of flagstone, concrete, or asphalt, should be checked for creaking, buckling, and other conditions dangerous to pedestrian travel.

Stone, brick, or concrete steps should be inspected for cracks, deterioration, and pointing.

Fences should be in a sound condition and painted. Fire escapes should be checked for paint condition, loose or broken treads and rails, proper operating condition, and proper connection to the house.

V. Noise as an Environmental Stress

People feel comfortable in an environment with a low-level, soothing, steady, unobstrusive level of sound, typical of the natural undisturbed environment. All of us have experienced the anguish that noise can cause, whether it be noise from a neighbor's television, the grinding of truck gears while asleep, the persistent whine of a fan motor, or the sound of children racing down the halls. These annoyances experienced in the home are producing public demands for noise control legislation.

Not only is noise disturbing, but studies also indicate that extreme noise can cause deafness and perhaps interfere with other bodily functions.

While few existing housing ordinances contain enforceable noise provisions, noise problems must be considered by the building inspector because they intimately affect and are affected by his decisions. As a housing inspector, you can help residents by suggesting corrective noise measures that can be taken; you can refer them to agencies, if needed, for corrective action; you can help them to understand that their noisy environment can place limitations on their behavior, capabilities, and satisfaction with their home.

Noise is unwanted sound. Noise can travel through air or through the building structure. The first stage of noise control is the control of sound at its source. If attempts to quiet the source are not completely successful, then other, more expensive corrective measures will be required.

Although a visual examination of a dwelling may detect some sources of noise leaks (see Figure 10) such as wide gaps or cracks at ceiling, floor, or adjoining wall edges, it is usually inadequate since it fails to detect sources of noise leaks hidden from the eye. A far more effective test is to be alert for the operation of some noisy device like a vacuum cleaner in a closed room and listen near the other side of the wall for any noise leakage. The ear is a reasonably good sensing device. If a noise leak is noticed, the partition may be surveyed at critical points with a bright flashlight while an observer looks for light leakage in a darkened room on the other side. Detection of any light leakage in the darkened room will signify a noise leak.

Noise carried as vibration by a building structure is called structure-borne noise. Detecting structure-borne noise caused by the operation of mechanical equipment is somewhat more difficult (see Figure 11). With noisy equipment in operation, the inspector can sometimes locate noise leaks or structure-borne noise paths by conducting similar hearing tests along with pressing the ear against various room surfaces or using fingertips to sense the vibration of these surfaces.

A Airborne Noise

The sources of airborne noise that cause the most frequent disturbances in the home are audio instruments such as televisions, radios, phonographs, or pianos; adults and children speaking loudly, singing, crying and shouting; household appliances such as garbage disposals, dishwashers, vacuum cleaners, clothes washers, and dryers; plumbing noises such as pipes knocking, toilets flushing, and water running.

The disturbing influences of airborne noise are generally limited to the areas near the noise source. For example, a phonograph may cause annoyance in rooms of a neighbor's apartment adjacent to the phonograph but rarely in rooms farther removed unless doors or passageways are left open. Sound absorption materials such as carpeting, acoustical tile, drapery, and upholstered furniture in the intervening rooms may often provide a significant reduction in the disturbing noise before it reaches rooms where quiet is desired.

Under no conditions should sound-absorptive materials be used on the surfaces of walls and ceilings for the sole purpose of preventing the transmission of sound as structure-borne noise. To do so would be a complete waste of effort. To illustrate, imagine the noise conducted by a wall constructed solely of drapery or acoustical tile attached to studs. The noise level in the room would be reduced, but sound produced in the room would pass through the wall to adjoining rooms with little, if any, reduction in noise level. Sound absorptive materials should be used in and near areas of high noise levels to limit airborne noise at the source of the noise and reduce the effects of noise along corridors.

The transmission of noise from one completely enclosed room to an adjoining room separated by a partition wall may be either direct transmission through the wall, indirect transmission through other walls, ceilings, and floors common to both rooms, or through corridors adjacent to such rooms.

In some older wood frame houses, the open troughs between studs and joists are efficient sound transmission paths. This noise transmission by indirect paths is known as "flanking transmission" (see Figure 10 and 11). In addition to the flanking paths, there may be noise leaks particularly along the ceiling, floor, and sidewall edges of the wall. In order to obtain the highest sound insulation performance, a partition wall must be of airtight construction. Care must be exercised to seal all openings, gaps, holes, joints, and penetrations of piping and conduits with a nonsetting caulking compound. Even hairline cracks, particularly at adjoining wall, floor, and ceiling edges, transmit a substantially greater amount of noise than would normally be expected on the basis of the size of the crack.

Figure 10. Flanking Transmission of Airborne Noise

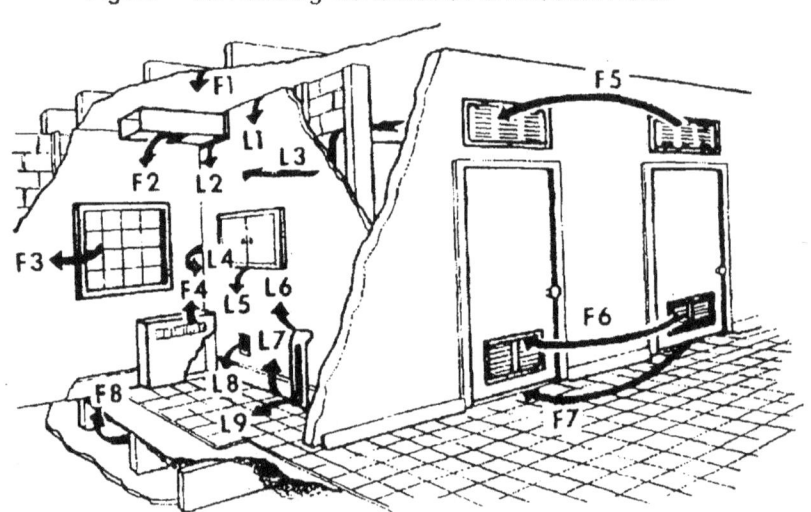

FLANKING NOISE PATHS	NOISE LEAKS
F1 Open plenums over walls, false ceilings	L1 Poor seal at ceiling edges
F2 Unbaffled duct runs	L2 Poor seal around duct penetrations
F3 Outdoor path, window to window	L3 Poor mortar joints, porous masonry block
F4 Continuous unbaffled inductor Units	L4 Poor seal at sidewall, filler panel, etc.
F5 Hall path, open vents	L5 Back-to-back cabinets, poor workmanship
F6 Hall path, louvered doors	L6 Holes, gaps at wall penetrations
F7 Hall path, openings under doors	L7 Poor seal at floor edges
F8 Open troughs in floor-ceiling structure	L8 Back-to-back electrical outlets
	L9 Holes, gaps at floor penetrations

Other points to consider are these: leaks are (a) batten strip A/O post connections of prefabricated walls, (b) under-floor pipe or service chases, (c) recessed, spanning light fixtures, (d) ceiling and floor cover plates of movable walls, (e) unsupported A/O unbacked wall-board joints (f) edges and backing of built-in cabinets and appliances, (g) prefabricated, hollow metal, exterior curtain walls.

It is often helpful to use one sound to drown out another disturbing noise; for example, music on the radio can be used to drown out the noise of traffic. The use of sound to drown out noise is particularly useful in masking noises that occur infrequently, such as accelerating or braking vehicles, periodic mechanical equipment noise, barking dogs, laughter, or shouting.

B **Structure-Borne Noise**

Structure-borne noise occurs when wall, floor, or other building elements are set into vibration by direct contact with vibrating sources such as mechanical equipment or domestic appliances. A small, vibrating pipe firmly attached to a plywood or gypsum wall panel will amplify the vibration noise. An illustration of this amplification of structure-borne noise is provided by the sound board of a piano. The major sources of structure-borne noise are the impact of walking on wood floors or of slamming doors, plumbing system noises, heating and air-conditioning system noises, noise from mechanical equipment or appliances, and vibration from sources outside the building. If the vibration is severe enough, it may have adverse effects not only on the occupants of a building but also on the building structure. Household appliances such as refrigerators, washing machines, sewing machines, clothes dryers, televisions, and pianos should be vibration isolated from the floor by means of rubber mounts placed under them if disturbing structure-borne noise is to be avoided. Residents should also be cautioned against locating these noise sources along party walls and in particular against mounting these appliances and kitchen cabinets directly on party walls so that the walls act as sounding boards in adjoining apartments. Window air-conditioners should be completely vibration isolated from the surrounding window frame by rubber gaskets and padding. The importance of isolating a vibrating source from the structure in the control of equipment noise cannot be overemphasized.

Another source of disturbing structure-borne noise is squeaking of wood floors. Some squeaks can be eliminated by lubricating the tongues of wood floor boards with mineral oil applied sparingly to the openings between adjacent boards. Loose finish flooring may be securely fastened to subflooring by surface nailing into the

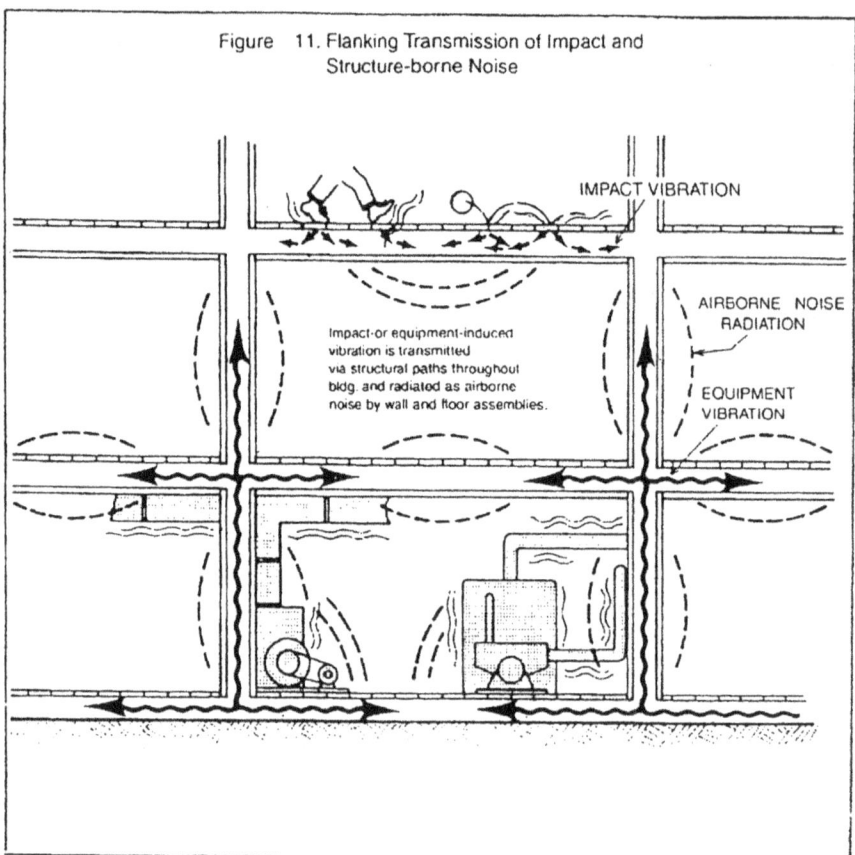

Figure 11. Flanking Transmission of Impact and Structure-borne Noise

subfloor and preferably the joists. Ring-type nails or sawtooth staples properly spaced should be used in nailing finish flooring to subflooring. In an exposed joist structure, where finish flooring is warped, driving screws up through the subfloor and into the finish floor will be effective in drawing the layers of flooring tightly together to reduce noise.

Of course, noise caused by the impact of walking or scraping can be substantially reduced by the use of carpets. In the case of door slams, the impact noise may be eliminated by the use of door closers or rubber bumpers.

The noisy hammering of a plumbing system is usually caused by the sudden interruption of water-flow, for example, by a quick closing or opening of a tap.

Air chambers can be built into the plumbing system to reduce water hammer. The air pockets, rubber inserts, or spring elements in air chambers act to reduce noise. Air chambers are explained in Chapter 6.

Defective, loose, or worn valve stems create intense chattering of the plumbing system. The defective device can frequently be found without difficulty, since immediate use of the device causes the vibration, which generally occurs at some low-flow-velocity setting and diminishes or disappears at a higher flow setting. For example, if a chattering noise occurs when a particular faucet or tap is opened partially and diminishes when fully opened, the faucet more than likely has some loose or defective parts and should be repaired.

Noise can be a very complex problem. The housing inspector is not expected to be an acoustics expert. Nor is he expected to be able to analyze and solve the noise problems that an acoustics consultant would normally handle. He can, however, help teach the public that the annoyances and stress caused by noise can be partially alleviated by a simple awareness of common noise problems found in many residences.

Although the housing inspector is not an expert in the fields of zoning, plumbing, building, and electrical systems, he should be familiar with the applicable code in each of the respective fields. Familiarization with these codes will better enable him to recognize violations.

www.ingramcontent.com/pod-product-compliance
Lightning Source LLC
Chambersburg PA
CBHW081822300426
44116CB00014B/2450